# HOW DOES TEACHER PAY COMPARE?

## Methodological Challenges and Answers

Sylvia A. Allegretto

Sean P. Corcoran

Lawrence Mishel

ECONOMIC POLICY INSTITUTE

## Acknowledgments

Economists Paul Scheible, Paul Carney, and Stephanie Boraas of the U.S. Bureau of Labor Statistics provided helpful information in the preparation of this report. Jin Dai and Danielle Gao did excellent work developing databases and data analyses. Richard Rothstein and David Wazeter provided useful comments, though they are not responsible for the ultimate outcome. Patrick Watson did a wonderful job editing, as usual. Grace Maro and Yulia Fungard ably provided research assistance. This project is part of the overall education research program at EPI.

ECONOMIC POLICY INSTITUTE
1660 L Street, NW, Suite 1200
Washington, D.C. 20036

http://www.epinet.org

ISBN: 1-932066-14-4

# Contents

# About the Authors

**Sylvia A. Allegretto** is an economist at the Economic Policy Institute. Her areas of research include unemployment, income inequality, and family budgets, and she is a co-author of *The State of Working America 2004-05*. She received a Ph.D. in economics from the University of Colorado at Boulder.

**Sean P. Corcoran** is an assistant professor of economics at California State University, Sacramento and a research associate of the Economic Policy Institute. His research interests include state and local public finance, the economics of education, and applied econometrics. His dissertation, on teacher quality and school finance, received the 2003 outstanding dissertation award from the American Education Finance Association and was recently featured in the "Economic Scene" column of *The New York Times*. Portions of this dissertation have been published in the *American Economic Review* and the *Journal of Policy Analysis and Management*.

**Lawrence Mishel** joined the Economic Policy Institute in 1987 and has been its president since 2002. His areas of research include wage determination, industrial relations, productivity and competitiveness, income inequality, and growth. He is the director of EPI's education research program, and has been a co-author of *The State of Working America* since the first version in 1988.

# The Debate Over Teacher Pay

Recent research in the economics of education has demonstrated the importance of individual teachers for students' academic success.[1] The No Child Left Behind Act of 2001 has raised the profile of the issue by requiring a qualified teacher in every classroom in 2005. Yet, mounting evidence suggests that many U.S. schools have found it increasingly difficult, except perhaps during the recent recession, to attract the very best candidates into the teaching profession.[2] As labor market opportunities have improved outside of teaching, public schools have lost the captive labor pool they once had with respect to women (who make up over 75% of all kindergarten through 12th grade teachers) and are today forced to compete with more lucrative professions for the best college graduates. The widespread desire in recent years to cut class sizes while simultaneously raising the quality of teachers (through such measures as No Child Left Behind) has made the recruiting task only that much more difficult.[3]

This concern over teacher quality has generated renewed interest in both the sufficiency of teacher pay to attract high-quality staff and the efficacy of various dimensions of teacher pay, including incentives and extra pay for working in particular fields or in particular locations (i.e., hard-to-staff schools).

For decades, researchers have asked whether teacher compensation has kept pace with outside job opportunities, and whether compensation is sufficiently competitive to attract the quality of instructors desired.[4] The importance of salaries (relative to other job characteristics, such as working conditions, summers off, and job flexibility) to the recruitment of high-quality teachers has also been studied in great detail. While the popular view is that teacher pay is relatively low and has not kept up with comparable professions over time, new claims suggest that teachers are actually well compensated when work hours, weeks of work, or benefits packages are taken into account.[5] Whatever the case, the many unique features of the teaching profession have almost certainly complicated efforts to compare its compensation to that of other professions.

In this report, we review recent analyses of relative teacher compensation, examine some of the ways in which the conclusions of these analyses differ, and provide our own detailed analysis of trends in the relative weekly pay of elementary and secondary school teachers. We propose a method for finding occupations comparable to the teaching profession based on specific job skill requirements, and compare teacher pay with pay in these professions as an additional way to track teachers' pay relative to that of comparable workers. We use hourly compensation and benefits data for teachers and professionals to estimate the extent of any "fringe benefit bias" that exists when comparisons of teacher wages are made without considering benefits, which frequently differ across professions. Last, we examine the data on hourly wages for teachers and other occupations found in the new National Compensation Survey (NCS), which is the basis for some new claims that teacher pay matches or exceeds the pay of comparable professions. Our examination of the NCS methodology for determining hourly wages concludes that it is an inappropriate source of data for comparing teacher pay to that of other professions.[6]

The major findings of our review and analysis include the following:

- Recent research shows that teacher quality is key to student and school success.

- A continuing issue is whether teacher pay is sufficient to attract and retain quality teachers: trends in relative teacher pay seem to coincide with trends in teacher quality over the long run.

- Several types of analyses show that teachers earn significantly less than comparable workers, and this wage disadvantage has grown considerably over the last 10 years.

- An analysis of weekly wage trends shows that teachers' wages have fallen behind those of other workers since 1996, with teachers' inflation-adjusted weekly wages rising just 0.8%, far less than the 12% weekly wage growth of other college graduates and of all workers.

- A comparison of teachers' weekly wages to those of other workers with similar education and experience shows that, since 1993, female teacher wages have fallen behind 13% and male teacher wages 12.5% (11.5% among all teachers). Since 1979 teacher wages relative to those of other similar workers have dropped 18.5% among women, 9.3% among men, and 13.1% among both combined.

- A comparison of teachers' wages to those of workers with comparable skill requirements, including accountants, reporters, registered nurses, computer programmers, clergy, personnel officers, and vocational counselors and inspectors, shows that teachers earned $116 less per week in 2002, a wage disadvantage of 12.2%. Because teachers worked more hours per week, the hourly wage disadvantage was an even larger 14.1%.

- Teachers' weekly wages have grown far more slowly than those for these comparable occupations; teacher wages have deteriorated about 14.8% since 1993 and by 12.0% since 1983 relative to comparable occupations.

- Although teachers have somewhat better health and pension benefits than do other professionals, these are offset partly by lower payroll taxes paid by employers (since some teachers are not in the Social Security system). Teachers have less premium pay (overtime and shift pay, for example), less paid leave, and fewer wage bonuses than do other professionals. Teacher benefits have not improved relative to other professionals since 1994 (the earliest data we have on benefits), so the growth in the teacher wage disadvantage has not been offset by improved benefits.

- The extent to which teachers enjoy greater benefits depends on the particular wage measure employed to study teacher relative pay. Based on a commonly used wage measure that is similar to the W-2 wages reported to the IRS (and used in our analyses), teachers in 2002 received 19.3% of their total compensation in benefits, slightly more than the 17.9% benefit share of compensation of professionals. These better benefits somewhat offset the teacher wage disadvantage but only to a modest extent. For instance, in terms of the roughly 14% hourly wage disadvantage for teachers we found relative to other workers of similar education and experience, an adjustment for benefits would yield a total compensation disadvantage for teachers of 12.5%, 1.5 percentage points less.

- The hourly wage data in the NCS, the relatively new Bureau of Labor Statistics survey, has been used in several recent analyses that found teacher wages to be on par with those of other professionals. Our examination of these data show that the vast differences in the way work time is measured in the NCS for teachers (K-12, as well as university professors, airline pilots, and others) and workers following a more traditional year-round schedule preclude an accurate comparison of teacher hourly wages relative to those of other professionals. These inconsistencies in work hour measurement (hours per week, weeks per year) in the NCS are so large as to obscure a 23.4% greater hourly wage advantage for professionals relative to K-12 teachers.

# CHAPTER I

# The Evidence on Teacher Pay and Teacher Quality

Instructional expenditure makes up far the largest share of aggregate K-12 public school spending in the United States. Expenditure on instruction in 1999-2000 totaled $200 billion, or over 60% of current expenditures on public schools (National Center for Education Statistics 2003, Table 164).

The long-run trend in average teacher pay is well documented. In 1956, the average K-12 teacher earned $27,139 per year (in 2002 dollars); by 2002, mean earnings had risen to $44,367 (a 63% increase in real earnings).[7] This growth in real salaries was by no means steady—the average teacher saw a larger than 15% *decline* in real annual earnings over the 1972-82 period ($41,769 to $35,318 in 2002 dollars), explained in part by the coincident decline in K-12 enrollment and a sharp reduction in the recruitment of new teachers. The trend is more dramatic when the changing demographics of teachers are taken into account.[8] By 1989, though, real average salaries had surpassed their 1972 level, and continued to rise through 2002, albeit at a slow rate (0.2% on an annual basis).

The evidence on how the compensation of teachers has fared *relative* to other professions is less clear. Such comparisons depend in part on how compensation is defined (for example, whether benefits are included or excluded from the calculation), on the pay interval (annual, weekly, or hourly) and on the reference group chosen (all workers, all college graduates, or specific professions). Recent analyses of relative teacher pay differ along all of these dimensions, as well as in their time frame and data source; not surprisingly, conclusions about changes in relative teacher pay can differ considerably depending on the methodology chosen.

Typical analyses of relative teacher compensation compare the trend in mean annual teacher pay with that of some comparison group.[9] This reference group may include all full-time workers, a certain class of workers (such as "white-collar professionals," or "government professionals"), full-time workers with at least a college degree, or specific professions. These studies tend to find that relative teacher pay rose until the early seventies; when real teacher salaries began to fall, so did their *relative* salaries (in other words, real teacher pay fell at a faster rate than that other professions, many of which also saw declines in real wages over this period). After some recovery in the 1980s, relative teacher pay began to fall again in the late 1980s and early 1990s, and has fallen steadily since. It should be noted, however, that teachers have not always earned less than other college graduates: female teachers, as recently as the 1950s, actually earned more on average than other female college graduates.[10]

Somewhat more sophisticated analyses of relative teacher pay attempt to control for differential changes in the demographic composition of the teaching and general workforces. The most notable divergence between these two populations occurred during the 1970s and 1980s, when the hiring of new teachers slowed and the average age and work experience of practicing teachers rose relative to other workers. Using data from the March Current Population Survey, Flyer and Rosen (1997) find that the earnings of the average teacher rose relative to those of college graduates between 1967 and 1989.[11] They note, however, that this increase can be attributed almost entirely to a higher rate of growth in the experience and education of the average teacher. After controlling for the demographic composition of the teaching and college graduate workforces, they find that the relative wage of elementary teachers fell more than 15% over this 20-year period. Bacolod (2003) and Hanushek and Rivkin (1997), using 1940-90 Census data and controlling for demographic changes in the workforce, find that the relative wage position of teachers has steadily eroded since 1960. Hanushek and Rivkin attribute nearly 70% of the overall relative wage drop to "pure" wage changes—changes in the relative wage due to shifts in the entire wage profile, not movements along this profile due to demographic shifts.

Some analyses of relative teacher compensation compare teacher pay directly to that of specific occupations. For example, the American Federation of Teachers (AFT), in its annual survey of teacher salaries, compares mean annual salaries of teachers to those of accountants, buyer and contract specialists, attorneys, computer systems analysts, engineers, and college professors.[12] The AFT finds that salaries in those occupations have remained consistently above those of teachers since the early 1960s (see Nelson and Drown 2003). In 2002, for example, accountants earned on average 23% more than teachers, computer systems analysts 68% more, and attorneys two times more. Teacher pay largely *gained* relative to these occupations through the 1970s and 1980s (although the trend wasn't steady), but began to fall in the early 1990s.[13] The selection of comparable occupations is usually quite unsystematic, however, and some disagreement arises from time to time over the choice of an appropriate comparison group. In a recent article in *Education Next,* for example, Podgursky (2003) argues that professions chosen as alternatives to teaching should be chosen more carefully; he suggests that journalists, registered nurses, military officers, and private school teachers might be more appropriate for making wage comparisons with teachers than attorneys, scientists, or computer programmers.

With all of the attention paid to relative teacher pay, it is reasonable to ask whether higher relative pay attracts better teachers, and in turn whether higher teacher pay translates into better educational outcomes for students. Unfortunately there is a lack of agreement over the appropriate measure of teacher quality;

the studies discussed below analyze a number of candidate measures of quality, including test scores, college selectivity, and relative pay.

Existing evidence on the relationship between teacher pay and teacher quality is divided. In the short-run, pay increases do not appear to have noticeable effects on the quality of candidates entering the teaching profession. Over the long run, however, trends in relative teacher pay seem to coincide with trends in teacher quality.

Ballou and Podgursky (1997), for example, find that increases in relative teacher salaries across states between 1979 and 1989 were not associated with increases in teacher quality (as measured by the relative SAT scores of prospective, but not necessarily actual, education majors in those states).[14] Figlio (2002) finds no statistically significant relationship between increases in district-level salaries in the short run and the quality of new hires in unionized school districts (where quality is measured using college selectivity). A handful of other studies (Figlio 1997; Chambers 1998; Hanushek, Kain, and Rivkin 1999; Murnane et al. 1991) find weak evidence that higher salaries attract better teachers, but, on the whole, the short-run evidence is mixed.

The long-run relationship between teacher pay and teacher quality is more striking. Recent research has shown that the most academically talented graduates became much less likely to choose teaching as a profession during the 1970s-80s period of decline in relative teacher pay.[15] Bacolod (2003) finds that declines in the relative quality of graduates entering the teaching profession were strongly associated with declines in relative teacher compensation that occurred throughout that time. Lakdawalla (2001, 2002) has postulated that rising productivity (and correspondingly higher wages) outside of the teaching profession has induced schools to substitute *quality* teachers (and the higher wages they would command) with a greater *quantity* of teachers (in an effort to create smaller class sizes), and he finds some empirical support for this hypothesis.[16]

The apparent relationship (at least in the long run) between teacher compensation and the recruitment of quality teachers is somewhat puzzling, given the longstanding conventional wisdom among some education economists that "money doesn't matter" to student outcomes (after all, nearly half of all school operating expenditures go to teachers).[17] However, two recent papers (Loeb and Page 2000 and Stoddard 2003) propose a convincing explanation: they note that studies which find no relationship between teacher salaries and student outcomes omit potentially important features of the teacher labor market that might be correlated with both salaries and student outcomes. For example, non-pecuniary job characteristics (like student quality) seem to be particularly important in teaching; these job characteristics are likely to vary widely across school districts or states and are likely to be "capitalized" into teacher wages as compensating differentials. In addition, alternative wage opportunities or local amenities may vary across districts or regions. Failure to adjust teacher salaries for these factors will confound estimates of the relationship between teacher pay and student outcomes.

Controlling for these job characteristics and local wage opportunities, Loeb and Page find that relative teacher pay in fact has a large effect on student outcomes (in their case, high-school dropout rates). Stoddard finds that once teacher salaries are adjusted for local amenities (whose value is reflected in the wages in other occupations) teacher pay is strongly correlated with student outcomes. [18]

The need for a careful, accurate assessment of a potential teacher's alternative wage, and how this compensation has changed over time, seems clear.

# CHAPTER II

# The Relative Weekly Earnings of Teachers

To present estimates of the trends in the relative weekly earnings of teachers since 1979,[19] we use data from the Bureau of Labor Statistics' Current Population Survey (CPS), specifically the Outgoing Rotation Groups (CPS-ORG) sample. The CPS, the monthly survey used by BLS to measure and report on unemployment, is based on a survey of about 60,000 households each month. The CPS-ORG data that we use include information on 145,000 workers each year (see Mishel et al. 2003, Wage Appendix, for further information). CPS data on wages, including the CPS-ORG data we use and the March CPS supplement that provides data on annual wages, provide the information most extensively used by economists to study wages and employment. (The CPS-ORG data are particularly useful because they contain information about wages earned "last week."[20]) Since 1994, the CPS-ORG survey has asked respondents to report their wages on a weekly, biweekly, monthly, or annual basis (whichever the respondent finds most appropriate): BLS uses information on weeks worked to derive the appropriate weekly wage. Respondents also report the hours they worked last week.

We restrict our sample to all full-time workers between the ages of 18 and 64.[21] We identify "teachers" using a three-digit Census occupation code, and include only elementary or secondary teachers (i.e., pre-kindergarten and kindergarten teachers, adult educators, and special education teachers are excluded).

One important innovation in our work is that we restrict our sample to those observations that do not have "imputed" wages. For a discussion of imputed wages, the problem they pose, and our methodology for working around this problem, see the box at right.

There are good reasons to evaluate teacher relative pay using either annual or weekly wages. While professional salaries are often compared on an annual basis, many have argued that the differences in weeks worked and weekly work hours between teachers and other professions do not permit an apples-to-apples comparison of annual pay.[22] Given that teachers typically receive summers off (and that they presumably value this additional leisure time, or the extra income they can earn during the summer), the comparison of annual wages is likely to *overstate* any teacher wage disadvantage. On the other hand, a comparison of weekly (or hourly) pay may *understate* a teacher wage disadvantage if teachers

# THE BIAS IN USING 'IMPUTED' WAGES

In the Current Population Survey, wages are imputed, or assigned, by the Census Bureau when a respondent fails to report wages. This practice creates a systematic and growing bias in comparing teachers to other professionals because: (1) teachers are assigned wages that are too high and non-teaching professionals are assigned wages too low, artificially reducing the wage gap between teachers and other professionals; and (2) the share of all observations that have imputed wages has risen sharply over the last 10 years.

The Census Bureau undertakes a careful and complicated process to impute wages. For our purposes here, the bottom line is that the process of imputing wages does not always take occupation into account. Thus, some non-teaching professionals have imputed wages that are based on teachers (and therefore are too low), and teachers have imputed wages that are frequently based on non-teaching professional wages (and are therefore too high). For example, teacher weekly wages in our full sample (using imputed and non-imputed observations) in 2003 were $900, 3.2% higher than the $872 in teacher weekly wages in a sample restricted to non-imputed observations. In contrast, the weekly wages of non-teacher college graduates was 2.1% lower in the full sample than in the sample with non-imputed observations ($1,128 versus $1,152). The inclusion of imputed observations, therefore, lowers the ratio of non-teacher weekly wages to teacher weekly wages among college graduates from 1.321 to 1.254, a considerable amount.

The share of observations having imputed wage data has increased remarkably: teacher imputations rose from 12.3% in 1983 to 15.1% in 1993 and to 26.3% in 2003, while among non-teacher college graduates imputations rose from 16.3% in 1983 to 17.9% in 1993 and to 33.0% in 2003. (The samples for these computations are full-time college graduates. There was a big jump in imputations associated with the redesign of the CPS-ORG between 1994 and 1996. Among all full-time college graduates, imputations rose from 17.6% of the ORG sample in 1993 to 23.4% in 1996.) The growing proportion of observations with imputed wages means that the bias in measuring teacher wages imparted by the imputations process has been growing over time. Consequently, imputations in the CPS-ORG are creating a systematic and growing bias in measuring teacher relative wages. As a result, we use only those observations of full-time workers with non-imputed wages.

Results using the full sample, with imputed and non-imputed wages, are available from the authors upon request.

Restricting the sample to non-imputed observations raises the issue of whether a selectivity arises that may bias our estimates. The issue can be thought of as whether there are systematic differences in which observations are given (or are in need of) imputed wages among teachers relative to non-teacher college graduates. We ran OLS and logit analyses that predicted being an imputed observation and included the same set of human capital variables we use for our estimates and a dummy variable for teachers. There did not seem to be any "teacher effect" except in a few years, and even then it was small. Experiments that interacted "teacher" with other variables did not show any systematic or significant (statistically or economically) interactions with "teacher." Also, these models had little explanatory power. We concluded that selectivity of the imputations does not present a problem for our estimates.

## Figure 1  Mean weekly wages of teachers, college graduates, and all workers, 1983-2003

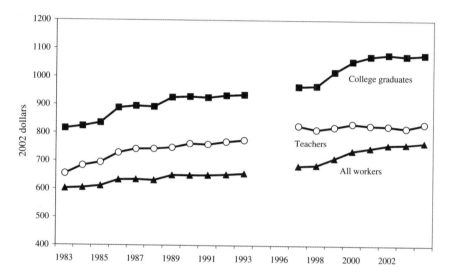

\* The redesign of the CPS boosted teacher wages relative to other wages, thereby making the data before and after 1994 not comparable.

Source: Authors' analysis of CPS data.

who desire to earn income over the summer cannot do so at the same rate of pay. Moreover, some teachers undertake professional training and prepare classroom materials and lessons in the summer and therefore think of themselves as full-year workers. Thus, any estimates of teacher relative wages for *weekly wages,* such as those we present, will understate teachers' disadvantage in the labor market.[23]

Some recent analyses of relative teacher hourly wages have used the National Compensation Survey (NCS), mentioned above, rather than the CPS used here. Using hourly wage data in the NCS holds the promise of comparing teacher wages without having to deal with the "summers off" issue. However, as we show later (in Chapter V), inconsistencies in measurement of weeks worked and weekly work hours between teachers and other professionals in the NCS do not allow for an accurate comparison of teacher and non-teacher hourly wages.

The mean weekly wage (in 2002 dollars) for all teachers, all workers, and all college graduates in the CPS from 1983 to 2003 are shown in **Figure 1** and in **Table 1** (Appendix A provides the data). There are no data shown for 1994 and 1995 because it is not possible in those years to identify which observations have imputed wages.[24] As is well known, college graduate wages rose faster than wages for all workers over this period. Teacher wages kept relative pace with those of

**Table 1 Weekly wages of teachers, non-teacher college graduates, and all workers 1983-2003**

| Year | Pooled | | | Female college graduates | | Male college graduates | |
|---|---|---|---|---|---|---|---|
| | All workers | College graduates | Teachers | Not teachers | Teachers | Not teachers | Teachers |
| **Weekly wages ($2002)** | | | | | | | |
| 1983 | $602 | $816 | $654 | $648 | $630 | $942 | $720 |
| 1989 | 649 | 926 | 747 | 750 | 725 | 1074 | 814 |
| 1993 | 656 | 936 | 775 | 793 | 759 | 1069 | 843 |
| 1996 | 682 | 965 | 826 | 828 | 809 | 1094 | 902 |
| 2003 | 766 | 1078 | 833 | 933 | 820 | 1246 | 899 |
| **Weekly wage growth** | | | | | | | |
| 1983-89 | 8.0% | 13.5% | 14.3% | 15.8% | 15.2% | 14.0% | 13.1% |
| 1989-93 | 1.0 | 1.1 | 3.6 | 5.7 | 4.7 | -0.5 | 3.6 |
| 1996-2003 | 12.3 | 11.8 | 0.8 | 12.7 | 1.3 | 13.9 | -0.3 |

Source: Authors' analysis of CPS data.

other college graduates over the 1983-89 period, each rising by about 14%. In the early 1990s (1989-93), teacher wages grew a bit faster than those of college graduates and other workers, 3.6% versus about 1.0%. Thereafter, teacher wages remained fairly flat while the wages of college graduates and other workers grew strongly and steadily. This chart suggests a steep erosion of teacher relative wages over the last 10 years.

Figure 1 shows a bump up in teacher wages between 1993 and 1996, which we attribute to a sharp rise in reported wages for teachers as result of a CPS redesign in 1994. Teacher weekly wages jumped 10.2% in nominal terms from 1993 to 1994, while the wages of other college graduates increased by just 2.2%. We believe this disparity in wage growth is due to the redesign in which, starting in 1994, respondents were able to provide wage information for periods that most suited them (hourly, weekly, biweekly, monthly, or annual rather than just "wages last week").[25] This change in wage measurement reduced the teacher wage gap by about eight percentage points. We examine the longer-run changes in teacher relative wages therefore by measuring changes over the period before 1993 and the period after 1996 so as to exclude the effect of the redesign on changes in relative wages.

Table 1 presents the growth in real weekly wages for teachers and for other college graduates for a pooled (male and female) sample as well as for men and women separately. These data show that teacher wage growth fell seriously behind that of other college graduates over the 1996-2003 period among both men and women. In particular, female teacher wages grew just 1.3% from 1996 to 2003, far less than the 12.7% growth among other female college graduates.[26]

**Figure 2** presents wage ratios (provided in Appendix Table B) constructed from these same CPS descriptive data to illustrate changes in mean teacher pay *relative* to that of all workers and to all college graduates. Teacher wages relative to other college graduates held steady over the 1983-93 period but declined sharply thereafter (excepting the redesign bump in the mid-1990s). Teacher wages fared better than those of all workers in the 1983-93 period, rising from 1.087 to 1.181 times that of other workers from 1983 to 1993. In contrast, this wage ratio fell 12 percentage points from 1996 to 2003.

**Figure 3** presents the ratio of the wages of teacher college graduates to those of other (non-teacher) college graduates for both men and women, again showing the steep erosion of teachers' relative weekly wages since 1996.

Estimates of teacher relative weekly wages that control for differences in education, experience, and other worker characteristics[27] are presented in **Table 2** and **Figure 4** for the pooled sample and for men and women (the year-by-year time series is presented in Appendix C). This "regression approach" yields a somewhat smaller erosion of the teacher relative wage since 1996 (a seven percentage-point drop) than that shown by the basic wage ratios (an 8.4 percentage-point drop relative to other college graduates; see Appendix B). Teacher wages fell relative to other comparable workers by a similar six percentage points among men as well as women (Table 2). For women teachers, the 6.3 percentage-point decline in their

**Figure 2  Ratio of teachers' weekly wages to workers and college graduates, 1983-2003**

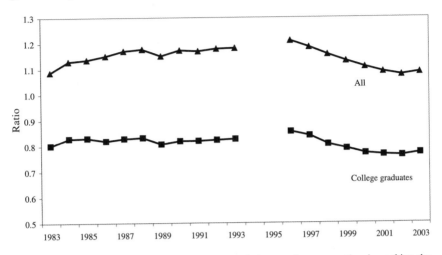

\* The redesign of the CPS boosted teacher wages relative to other wages, thereby making the data before and after 1994 not comparable.

Source: Authors' analysis of CPS data.

**Figure 3  Ratio of teachers' weekly wages to other college graduates, by gender, 1983-2003**

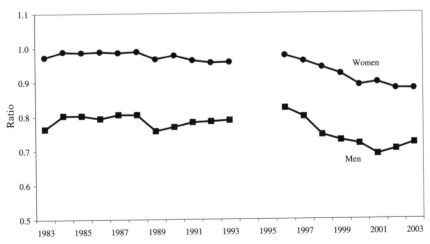

\* The redesign of the CPS boosted teacher wages relative to other wages, thereby making the data before and after 1994 not comparable.

Source: Authors' analysis of CPS data.

## Table 2 Regression-adjusted teachers' relative wages, 1979-2003

| Year | Estimated teacher relative weekly wage* | | |
| --- | --- | --- | --- |
| | Pooled | Women | Men |
| 1979 | -6.8% | 2.9% | -22.1% |
| 1989 | -9.2 | -1.4 | -21.6 |
| 1993 | -8.5 | -2.6 | -18.9 |
| 1996** | -6.6 | -2.6 | -16.9 |
| 2003 | -13.6 | -8.9 | -23.1 |

*Changes in the regression-adjusted relative wage*

| | | | |
| --- | --- | --- | --- |
| 1979-93 | -1.7 | -5.5 | 3.2 |
| 1993-96*** | -4.5 | -6.7 | -6.3 |
| 1996-2003 | -7.0 | -6.3 | -6.2 |
| 1979-2003 | -13.1 | -18.5 | -9.3 |

\* Teachers' weekly wage relative to other workers controlling for education, age as a quartic, region, marital status, and race/ethnicity.

\*\* Data for 1994 and 1995 not available because imputed wages cannot be identified.

\*\*\* Based on annual wage regressions using the March CPS.

Source: Authors' analysis of CPS data.

relative wage is on top of the 5.5 percentage-point erosion among women in the earlier 1979-93 period. In contrast, male teachers saw their relative wages improve in this earlier period by 3.2 percentage points. Because of the CPS redesign, the CPS-ORG data cannot be used to estimate the change in the teacher relative wage from 1993 to 1996 (recall also that we cannot identify the imputed observations in 1994 and 1995).[28] However, Table 2 employs the same methodology using March CPS data on annual wages to show the change in the teacher relative wage from 1993 to 1996 (the wage questions in this part of the CPS were not affected by the redesign). These results show that the steep erosion of teacher relative wages began as early as 1993, with the estimates showing a 4.5 percentage-point erosion from 1993 to 1996. Looking at the results for 1993-96 and 1996-2003 together shows an erosion of teacher relative wages among men and women combined of 11.5 percentage points and of women and men, respectively, of 13.0 and 12.5 percentage points. Over the entire 1983-2003 period, teacher relative wages have eroded 13.1 percentage points overall, 18.5 percentage points among women and 9.3 percentage points among men.

Our estimates show that, in 2003, teachers had 13.6% lower weekly wages than other comparable workers. Among men, teachers earned 23.1% less and, among women, teachers earned 8.9% less.

**Figure 4 Estimated teacher relative weekly wage, 1979-2003**

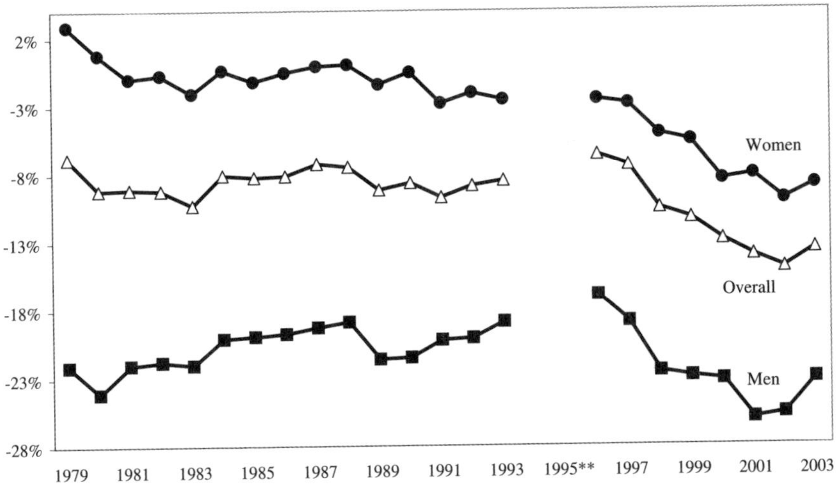

Data for 1994 and 1995 not available because imputed wages cannot be identified.

Source: Authors' analysis of CPS data.

As mentioned in Chapter I, however, the demographic characteristics of the average teacher changed relative to that of the average worker and average college graduate over this 30-year period. This change motivated Flyer and Rosen (1997) to estimate teachers wages relative to college graduates holding demographics constant at those exhibited by the average teacher in an earlier (or alternatively, a later) year. Their methodology uses separate regressions for male and female teachers and other workers to allow teachers and other workers to have different returns to education, experience, and other factors.[29] We used the Flyer and Rosen methodology as a check on our results and found an even larger erosion of teacher relative wages over the last 10 years and a larger teacher wage disadvantage in 2003. These results did not change when we switched from an earlier year's to a later year's mix of workforce characteristics.[30]

We experimented with some other specifications for estimating regression-adjusted teacher relative wages; our results sometimes showed a larger teacher wage disadvantage, as did the Flyer and Rosen methodology, and always showed an erosion of the teacher relative wage at least as large as the seven percentage-point erosion we have identified for the 1996-2003 period.[31] We have also conducted some preliminary analysis of which teachers saw the greatest and least erosion of their relative wage. One important finding from this preliminary work is that the greatest relative wage erosion was among older teachers and the least erosion was among young teachers.[32] Last, we conducted our analysis of teacher relative wages using a measure of hourly wages from the CPS-ORG data. This method allows a change in relative weekly hours between teachers and comparable workers to affect the relative wage estimates. We found a somewhat larger teacher wage disadvantage for hourly wages (-16.0 %) than weekly wages (-13.6%) in 2003 and a larger erosion (about two percentage points more) of teacher relative wages since 1996.

# CHAPTER III

# Identifying Occupations Comparable to Teaching

In Chapter II we compared the weekly pay of school teachers to two broad classes of workers—all full-time non-teachers and all college graduates—using broad comparisons and breakdowns that control for worker characteristics such as experience, region, and race. However, teacher salaries are frequently, and usefully (for a longer time series or for comparisons at a local or state level), compared directly with those of specific professions thought to be comparable to teaching.[33] Unfortunately, these professions are chosen based on limited data availability or are chosen somewhat arbitrarily without reference to any selection criteria.[34] Researchers have not been able to systematically identify professions that represent proper comparison groups to the teaching profession. In this section, we use new occupational "skill level" data from the Bureau of Labor Statistics' NCS to identify professions that are similar to teaching in the specific skills used on the job. As explained below, we identify 16 professions that we argue are comparable to teaching based both on their raw skill requirements and upon the market valuation of these skills. We then compare the weekly wages, weekly hours, and hourly wages of teachers with this group of 16 occupations.[35]

As part of the NCS, the BLS collects specific occupational skill information (via field visits to establishments employing roughly 84 million workers) for a sample of occupations within each surveyed establishment. Each occupation studied in an establishment is rated for the level of skill required along 10 different dimensions (or "generic leveling factors," as the BLS refers to them). **Table 3** lists these 10 factors, the BLS description of each, and the number of skill levels within each leveling factor. Because work within a particular occupation will differ across establishments (e.g., requiring more or less "knowledge" or "complexity"), each occupation, at the national aggregate, has a *distribution* of skills under each generic leveling factor. For example, among accountant jobs surveyed, 75% may require a knowledge level of 9, 10% may require a knowledge level of 8, and so on. Levels within each criterion are defined quite specifically, so that occupations can be accurately scored by BLS analysts.

Pierce (1999) uses these occupational skill distributions as independent variables in a series of wage breakdowns, and finds that these generic leveling factors explain a large proportion of the variance in wages across occupations,

## Table 3. NCS occupational leveling criteria

**KNOWLEDGE** *(Factor levels: 9; possible points: 1,850)* measures the nature and extent of information or facts that the workers must understand to do acceptable work (e.g., steps, procedures, practices, rules, policies, theories, principles, and concepts) and the nature and extent of the skills needed to apply those knowledges. To be used as a basis for selecting a level under this factor, knowledge must be required and applied.

**SUPERVISION RECEIVED** *(Factor levels: 5; possible points: 650)* covers the nature and extent of direct or indirect controls exercised by the supervisor, the employee's responsibility and the review of completed work.

**GUIDELINES** *(Factor levels: 5; possible points; 650)* covers the nature of guidelines and the judgment needed to apply them. Guides used include, for example: desk manuals, established procedures and policies, traditional practices, and reference materials such as dictionaries, style manuals, engineering handbooks, and the pharmacopoeia.

**COMPLEXITY** *(Factor levels: 6; possible points: 450)* covers the nature, number, variety, and intricacy of tasks, steps, processes, or methods in the work performed; the difficulty in identifying what needs to be done; and the difficulty and originality involved in performing the work..

**SCOPE AND EFFECT** *(Factor levels: 6; possible points: 450)* covers the relationship between the nature of the work, i.e., the purpose, breadth, and depth of the assignment, and the effect of work products or services both within and outside the organization. Effect measures such things as whether the work output facilitates the work of others, provides timely services of a personal nature, or impacts on the adequacy of research conclusions.

**PERSONAL CONTACTS** *(Factor level: 4; possible points: 110)* includes face-to-face contacts and telephone and radio dialogue with persons not in the supervisory chain. Levels described under this factor are based on what is required to make the initial contact, the difficulty of communicating with those contacted, and the setting in which the contact takes place (e.g., the degree to which the employee and those contacted recognize their relative roles and authorities).

**PURPOSE OF CONTACTS** *(Factor levels: 4; possible points: 220)* ranges from factual exchanges of information to situations involving significant or controversial issues and differing viewpoints, goals, or objectives. The personal contacts that serve as the basis for the level selected for this factor must be the same as the contacts that are the basis for the level selected for Factor 6.

**PHYSICAL DEMANDS** *(Factor levels: 3; possible points: 50)* covers the requirements and physical demands placed on the employee by the work assignment. This includes physical characteristics and abilities and the physical exertion involved in the work.

**WORK ENVIRONMENT** *(Factors levels: 3; possible points: 50)* considers the risks and discomforts in the employee's physical surroundings or the nature of the work assignment and the safety regulations required.

**SUPERVISORY DUTIES** *(Factor levels: 6; possible points: 0)* describes the level of supervisory responsibility for a position.

Source: Appendices C and D, U.S. DOL (2003).

**Table 4 Descriptive statistics for skill summary measures**

|  | Points | Market Value |
|---|---|---|
| Average | 1216 | 0.586 |
| Standard deviation | 692 | 0.379 |
| Median | 1065 | 0.505 |
| Maximum | 3853 | 1.804 |
| Minimum | 252 | 0.029 |
| K-12 teachers | 1752 | 0.936 |
| Number of occupations | 426 | 426 |

Source: Authors' analysis of NCS data.

even in the presence of "traditional" factors or covariates (firm size, unionization, etc).[36] In particular, Pierce finds that 75% of the variance in wages can be explained with generic leveling factors alone. The leveling factors are also effective in explaining variation in hourly wages *within* white-collar occupations. Thus, it appears the skill ratings developed by BLS reflect skills that are valued in the marketplace.

We employ two summary measures of overall skill for each occupation—a "point" measure and a "market value" measure. The construction of these measures is detailed in the accompanying box detailed in the box on the next page.

The descriptive statistics for these two summary measures of occupation skill are presented in **Table 4**, along with the skill ratings for K-12 teachers. Teachers seem to have skills that are one standard deviation above the median of all occupations, whether looking at the point measure or market value measure.

Based on these two summary measures of occupational skill, we identify 16 professional and managerial occupations that we believe to be comparable to K-12 teachers (that is, these occupations were found to have similar skill ratings as teachers using both measures).[37] This list of comparable occupations is presented in **Table 5**, along with their point and market value measures. We have also included average weekly wages from the CPS-ORG for each occupation.[38] Each occupation's share of total employment among these 16 comparable occupations is presented in the last column; we use these shares to create a composite index of comparable occupations. By design, both the point value and the market value of skills are essentially equivalent for the teacher and the comparable occupations.

This list of comparable occupations was developed empirically, but it has an intuitive plausibility, at least to us. The eight largest occupations in this group—accountants, reporters, registered nurses, computer programmers, clergy, personnel officers, vocational counselors, and inspectors—make up 92% of these 16

## COMPUTING 'SKILL MEASURES' TO ASSESS COMPARABLE JOBS

The "point" and "market value" skill measures are based on Pierce's estimated returns to skill within each generic leveling factor, the distribution of employment across skill levels within each occupation, and a "point rating system" for skill levels. The point measure is based on the federal government's "factor evaluation system" used to rate white-collar jobs within the public sector. Points are assigned to higher skill levels within each skill dimension (the total possible points for each dimension are given in Table 3); some skill dimensions (such as knowledge) are weighted more heavily than others (such as complexity). In this point system the weighting of factors is based on the assumptions built into the factor evaluation system, but they generally reflect market valuations to some extent. Note that no points are given for the 10th factor, supervision, which is not part of the federal system. Total points for each occupation in the NCS were provided to the authors by the BLS from an unpublished tabulation. These data allow us to compute summary measures of overall skill for each occupation and identify occupations that have comparable skills (and skills similarly valued by the marketplace) to teaching. Each of Pierce's coefficients are an estimate of the wage premium associated with being in an occupation requiring that particular skill level, relative to an occupation with the lowest level of that skill (all else held constant). For example, the coefficient estimate on "complexity level 4" of 0.096 suggests that a worker in an occupation requiring a complexity level of 4 can expect to receive 9.6% higher wages than a worker in an occupation with complexity level 1, all else equal. The largest wage premiums are for occupations requiring high levels of knowledge, little oversight, high complexity, and supervisory responsibilities.

The market value measure is intended to capture the market value of the skills required by each occupation, and was computed as follows:

$$\hat{w}_j = \sum_{i=1}^{9} \sum_{k=1}^{K_j} \hat{\beta}_{ik} \, q_{jik}$$

In this expression, the $\hat{\beta}_{ik}$ are Pierce's (1999) estimated wage premiums for skill dimension $i$ (such as "knowledge") and skill level $k$ (there are $K_i$ skill levels within generic leveling factor $i$), and the $q_{jik}$ are the proportion of jobs in occupation $j$ that require the skill level $ik$. Thus, $\hat{w}_j$ is the predicted (log) wage premium commanded by the skills used in occupation $j$, taking into account the distribution of skill requirements within an occupation $j$. This wage premium is defined relative to a "counterfactual" occupation where all employment is at the lowest skill rating for each factor. In non-technical terms, this market value measure of skills essentially draws on information that identifies how much more in wages workers with particular skill levels earn and then uses information on the skill levels of each occupation to calculate how much more workers in that occupation earn compared to other occupations where workers have different skills. This method provides a ranking of occupations.

**Table 5  Comparable occupations to teachers**

| Occ. Code | Occupation | Skill rating/leveling factors | | Weekly wages (2002)* | Employment share |
|---|---|---|---|---|---|
| | | Points | Market value | | |
| 23 | Accountants and auditors | 1,689 | 0.900 | 932 | 25.9% |
| 24 | Underwriters | 1,767 | 0.940 | 942 | 1.9% |
| 27 | Personnel- training and labor relations specialists | 1,764 | 0.932 | 915 | 8.6% |
| 36 | Inspectors and compliance officers, except construction | 1,739 | 0.922 | 937 | 4.3% |
| 43 | Architects | 1,822 | 0.962 | 1,116 | 2.1% |
| 79 | Forestry and conservation scientists | 1,829 | 0.968 | 944 | 0.5% |
| 95 | Registered nurses | 1,769 | 0.956 | 942 | 27.7% |
| 99 | Occupational therapists | 1,782 | 0.951 | 913 | 0.7% |
| 103 | Physical therapists | 1,859 | 0.988 | 1,004 | 1.5% |
| 148 | Trade and industrial teachers | 1,810 | 0.950 | 1,248 | 0.1% |
| 163 | Vocational and educational counselors | 1,821 | 0.960 | 889 | 4.1% |
| 165 | Archivists and curators | 1,782 | 0.967 | 909 | 0.4% |
| 176 | Clergy | 1,855 | 0.971 | 699 | 5.6% |
| 184 | Technical writers | 1,846 | 0.977 | 1,052 | 1.2% |
| 195 | Editors and reporters | 1,711 | 0.921 | 929 | 4.3% |
| 229 | Computer programmers | 1,727 | 0.875 | 1,171 | 11.3% |
| | **Average** | 1,786 | 0.946 | 971 | 100.0% |
| | **Weighted average, comparables** | 1,750 | 0.929 | 952 | |
| | *Teachers* | | | | |
| 157 | Secondary school teachers | 1,757 | 0.939 | 874 | 38.6% |
| 158 | Teachers, special education | 1,776 | 0.950 | 820 | 8.9% |
| 156 | Elementary school teachers | 1,743 | 0.932 | 811 | 52.5% |
| | **Weighted average, teachers** | 1,752 | 0.936 | 845 | 100.0% |

* CPS average weekly wages for full-time workers.

Source: Authors' analysis.

## Table 6 Comparison of teachers and comparable occupations, 2002

|  | Weekly wages | Weekly hours | Hourly wages |
|---|---|---|---|
| Occupation: |  |  |  |
| Comparables (composite) | $952.30 | 42.4 | $23.06 |
| Teachers | 836.00 | 43.9 | 19.82 |
| Difference | $-116.30 | 1.5 | $-3.24 |
| Difference (%) | -12.2% | 3.5% | -14.1% |

*Employment-weighted averages of comparable occupations and of K-12 teacher occupations.

Source: Authors' analysis.

occupations' total employment and include many of the occupations frequently cited as comparable to teaching.

**Table 6** presents a comparison of the weekly wages, weekly hours, and hourly wages of these comparable occupations and of teachers in 2002.[39] The results show that teachers earned $116 less per week than those in comparable occupations, a wage disadvantage of 12.2%. Because teachers worked more hours, the hourly wage disadvantage is an even larger 14.1%.

We now turn to an analysis of trends over time in teacher wages relative to these comparable occupations. **Table 7** presents the weekly wages for teachers and for the 16 comparable occupations over the 1983-2002 period.[40]

As we discussed with the earlier estimates using the CPS weekly wage data, the CPS redesign creates a discontinuity in 1994—the redesign raised teacher wages relative to other occupations. We also do not have data for 1994 and 1995 because there are no flags indicating that observations have imputed, or allocated, wages in 1994 and the flag is available for only four months in 1995. Thus, as with the regression estimates, Table 7 computes the change of relative wages from 1983 to 2002 as the sum of the 1983-93 change and the 1996-2002 change. We again use the change in teacher relative wages found using the March CPS data as our estimate of what occurred over the 1993-96 period. This corrects as best we can for the shift due to the 1994 redesign and the fact that we cannot identify imputed observations in the CPS-ORG data in 1994 and through most of 1995.

Specifically, the teacher relative wage disadvantage grew steeply over the 1996-2002 period by 10.4%, while the teacher relative wage declined over the 1983-93 period by 2.8%. Obtaining an estimate of the change in the teacher relative wage over the entire 1983-2002 requires an estimate for the 1993-96 period (for which we do not have CPS weekly wage data). In our analysis in Chapter II we used the 4.5 percentage-point erosion of teacher relative wages over

**Table 7 Change in weekly wages, teachers and comparable occupations, 1983-2002**

|  | Weekly wages Comparable occupations | Weekly wages Teachers | Teachers relative to comparables |
|---|---|---|---|
| 1983 | $431.23 | $384.24 | -10.9% |
| 1984 | 457.18 | 415.33 | -9.2 |
| 1985 | 472.98 | 438.80 | -7.2 |
| 1986 | 501.94 | 466.91 | -7.0 |
| 1987 | 526.88 | 496.02 | -5.9 |
| 1988 | 551.04 | 521.56 | -5.3 |
| 1989 | 593.63 | 551.42 | -7.1 |
| 1990 | 623.89 | 580.16 | -7.0 |
| 1991 | 652.36 | 600.22 | -8.0 |
| 1992 | 681.96 | 621.05 | -8.9 |
| 1993 | 703.20 | 646.43 | -8.1 |
| **CPS data redesign\*** |  |  |  |
| 1994 | \*\* | \*\* | \*\* |
| 1995 | \*\* | \*\* | \*\* |
| 1996 | 734.31 | 720.71 | -1.9 |
| 1997 | 758.34 | 735.86 | -3.0 |
| 1998 | 796.92 | 752.82 | -5.5 |
| 1999 | 839.98 | 769.77 | -8.4 |
| 2000 | 875.83 | 790.70 | -9.7 |
| 2001 | 907.14 | 811.68 | -10.5 |
| 2002 | 952.28 | 835.99 | -12.2 |
| Change |  |  |  |
| 1983-93 |  |  | 2.8% |
| 1993-96\*\*\* |  |  | -4.5 |
| 1996-2002 |  |  | -10.4 |
| Total |  |  | -12.0 |

\*    CPS redesign causes data before 1994 to be not comparable to data for 1994 and beyond.

\*\*   No data for 1994 because allocated observations not identified; only 25% of allocated data in 1995 are identified.

\*\*\* Based on annual wage regressions using the March CPS.

Source: Authors' analysis.

the 1993-96 period estimated using annual wages from the March CPS as the proxy for what happened in this period. Doing so again for this analysis suggests that teacher wages relative to those of comparable occupations have deteriorated about 16.4% since 1993 or by 13.5% since 1983.

The post-1996 erosion of teachers' weekly wages was greater relative to comparable occupations (a drop of 10.4 percentage points) than relative to other college graduates using individual worker data, controlling for demographic characteristics (a drop of about 7.0 percentage points).

# CHAPTER IV

# The 'Fringe Benefit Bias'

Our analysis of relative teacher compensation thus far has focused entirely on the wages of teachers relative to other workers. Yet, fringe benefits such as pensions and health insurance are an increasingly important component of the total compensation package. Many observers argue that teachers enjoy more attractive fringe benefit packages than other professionals, suggesting that our measure of relative teacher pay overstates the teacher disadvantage in total compensation.[41]

In this section, we examine whether and how much our estimates of relative teacher pay should be adjusted to reflect differences in total compensation. That is, we will attempt to measure the size of the "fringe benefit bias."

We are not aware of any prior estimates of the fringe benefit bias, although the data are readily available. Most analysts simply note that benefits are a sizable part of total compensation, and they reiterate the popular assumption that teachers' benefits packages are more attractive than those of comparable professions (thus implying a fringe benefit bias in relative wage comparisons). Vedder (2003) attempts a quantitative assessment but makes a conceptual error in doing so. Vedder (2003, 16) raises the benefit issue as follows: "If direct hourly compensation [wages] averages perhaps five to eight percent more for teachers than for all professional workers, and fringe benefits are perhaps five percent more, all told, teachers' average hourly compensation [wages] plus benefits exceeds the average for all professionals by roughly 10 to 15%." Note that Vedder mistakenly *adds* his assumed relative wage difference to a teacher relative fringe benefit difference. Vedder's methodology mistakenly concludes a much different bias—larger in size, and of the wrong sign.[42]

**Table 8** provides total compensation shares from the Bureau of Labor Statistics' Employer Costs for Employee Compensation (ECEC) series. These data capture employer costs from all levels of government, both state and local where relevant. We use these data to compute the fringe benefit bias for two years—1994 and 2002—and see how the bias has changed (if at all) over this eight-year period.[43] These estimates, in turn, will allow us to assess whether the growing teacher wage disadvantage we have found over this period was partially offset or exaggerated by a change in teachers' benefits relative to other workers.

Table 8 divides total compensation into several categories of pay, including wages, benefits, and payroll taxes. "Wages" are, in turn, divided into two groups. The first is "basic wages," which are defined by the BLS as "regular payments from

**Table 8 Shares of total compensation, teachers and professionals**

| | 1994 | | 2002 | |
|---|---|---|---|---|
| | Teachers | Professionals | Teachers | Professionals |
| Basic wages | 75.3% | 73.3% | 75.3% | 73.6% |
| Other wages: premiums and paid leave | 4.8 | 8.0 | 5.4 | 8.5 |
| Total W-2 wages | 80.0 | 81.3 | 80.7 | 82.1 |
| Health and pension benefits | 14.5 | 12.2 | 13.5 | 11.3 |
| Payroll taxes | 5.5 | 6.5 | 5.8 | 6.5 |
| Total compensation | 100.0 | 100.0 | 100.0 | 100.0 |
| Ratio: W-2 wages to basic wages | 1.063 | 1.109 | 1.072 | 1.116 |
| Ratio: total compensation to W-2 wages | 1.249 | 1.230 | 1.239 | 1.218 |
| Ratio: total compensation to basic wages | 1.329 | 1.364 | 1.328 | 1.359 |

Note: "basic wages" are those published by the National Compensation Survey; "W-2 wages" are comparable to those published by the Current Population Survey.

Source: U.S. Department of Labor (2000; 2004c).

the employer to the employee as compensation for straight-time hourly work, or for any salaried work performed." This definition of wages is what the ECEC and the NCS label as wages, and is what those who have used these data (Podgursky 2003, Vedder 2003) have analyzed. This definition excludes the second group, "other wages," which includes premium pay for overtime, paid leave, and profit-sharing. The sum of basic and other wages is identified as "Total W-2 wages"; this measure corresponds to the wage measure used in the CPS and corresponds to the wages received in weekly (or biweekly) paychecks. W-2 wages are also what employers report to the Internal Revenue Service. It is important to note that one will obtain a different teacher wage differential depending on which wage measure is employed; this follows from the fact that "other wages" are a larger part of compensation for other professionals (8.5% in 2002) than for teachers (5.4%), since teachers rarely receive bonuses or paid vacation, although they may receive additional wages for extracurricular activities. Consequently, analysis of basic wages alone will tend to understate the teacher wage differential, relative to an analysis of total (W-2) wages, by approximately 3.5 percentage points.

Table 8 also presents the shares of the two non-wage (or fringe benefit) components of compensation—health and pension benefits and payroll taxes (Social Security, unemployment insurance, and workers' compensation). Teachers have a greater share of their compensation in health and pension benefits, which made up 13.5% of their compensation and 11.3% of professional compensation in 2002. One reason these costs are greater is that teacher health benefits are provided for the full year for workers who receive salaries for less than a full year.[44] These greater costs would also reflect teachers having better benefit packages.[45] Note that payroll taxes are less for teachers, probably because some teachers do not participate in the Social Security system. Non-wage compensation as a whole was more important for teachers (19.3%) than for professionals (17.9%).

Another way to summarize the differences in fringe benefits is to note, as we show in Table 8, that total compensation exceeded W-2 wages by 23.9% for teachers and by 21.8% for professionals. This suggests that there is a positive benefits bias when analyzing W-2 wages (as we do in Chapter II with the CPS and with comparable occupations in Chapter III), so that the teachers' relative wage disadvantage we have identified would in fact be smaller if we had information on total compensation. In contrast, the difference between total compensation and *basic wages* is larger for professionals than for teachers; an analysis with basic wages would tend to *understate* the relative teacher disadvantage in total compensation.

In **Table 9**, we use the data in Table 8 to simulate the benefits bias for each measure of wages—basic and total (W-2). The analysis is presented for both 1994 and 2002 so that we can identify any potential changes in this bias over time. We assume a negative teacher wage differential of 14% (i.e., teachers earn 14% less in wages than other professionals) and compute what the comparable differential would be for total compensation, given the data in Table 8. The difference between the wage differential and the compensation differential is the benefits bias.[46]

## Table 9 Estimating the benefits bias for W-2 and basic wages measures

|  | 1994 | 2002 |
|---|---|---|
| **W-2 wages** | | |
| *W-2 wage gap (comparables=100)** | | |
| Teachers | 86.0 | 86.0 |
| Comparables | 100.0 | 100.0 |
| | | |
| *Compensation* | | |
| Teachers | 107.5 | 106.6 |
| Comparables | 123.0 | 121.8 |
| | | |
| *Compensation rescaled*** | | |
| Teachers | 87.4 | 87.5 |
| Comparables | 100.0 | 100.0 |
| "Benefit bias"*** | 1.4 | 1.5 |

|  | 1994 | 2002 |
|---|---|---|
| **Basic wages** | | |
| *Basic wage gap (comparables=100)** | | |
| Teachers | 86.0 | 86.0 |
| Comparables | 100.0 | 100.0 |
| | | |
| *Compensation* | | |
| Teacher | 114.3 | 114.2 |
| Comparables | 136.4 | 135.9 |
| | | |
| *Compensation rescaled*** | | |
| Teacher | 83.8 | 84.1 |
| Comparables | 100.0 | 100.0 |
| | | |
| Benefit and other wage "bias"*** | -2.2 | -1.9 |

\* The 14% teacher wage gap/disadvantage is an assumption, used for illustrative purposes. A different assumption would lead to comparable results.

\*\* Rescaled so that comparables equal 100.

\*\*\* "Benefit bias" is the percentage-point difference between the teachers' wage (dis)advantage and the comparable (dis)advantage in total compensation.

Source: Authors' analysis.

For the most common measure of wages, W-2 wages, a 14% teacher wage disadvantage in 2002 is equivalent to a 12.5% teacher total compensation disadvantage. This difference implies a benefit bias of 1.5 percentage points in 2002. We find a similar benefit bias in 1994 of 1.4 percentage points, suggesting that the erosion of teacher wages relative to their comparables we found in Chapters II and III has not been offset by any gain by teachers in their relative benefits.

As discussed above, using the basic wages measure in the NCS yields a different benefit bias. For basic wages in 2002, a 14% teacher wage disadvantage is equivalent to 15.9% teacher total compensation disadvantage, a negative benefit bias of 1.9 percentage points. Thus, studies using a basic wage measure *overstate* teachers' pay (understate the teacher pay disadvantage) relative to others compared to what an analysis of total compensation would show. This bias is attributable to a basic wages measure of wages that does not include information on "other wages," including paid leave and wage bonuses that teachers tend to have less of than other professionals. The fringe benefit bias for basic wages was a bit smaller in 2002 than in 1994 (falling from -2.2 to -1.9). Studies using a basic wage measure of wages such as in the NCS do indeed have a fringe benefit bias, but not the one they claim (see Podgursky 2003 and Vedder 2003): NCS data on wages overstate teachers' full compensation relative to other professionals and thereby provide comparisons that overstate teacher pay relative to other professionals.

# CHAPTER V

# Comparing Measures of Weekly Wages in the NCS vs. the CPS

As we discussed in Chapter I, conclusions regarding relative teacher pay are dependent on data source, reference group, and pay interval. In this section, we briefly compare and contrast two data sources provided by the Bureau of Labor Statistics—the National Compensation Survey and the Current Population Survey—that have been used to make occupational salary comparisons. We find that large differences in the way in which working hours and wages of teachers and non-teachers are reported in the NCS have a strong influence on the measurement of relative teacher pay. Consequently, it is inappropriate to use NCS data on hourly or weekly wages to compare teachers' wages to those of other workers. The BLS economist that oversees the NCS methodology has expressed a comparable caution in the use of NCS hourly wage data, as we discuss below.

The NCS is a nationally representative random sample of jobs in the non-agriculture, non–federal government economy.[47] Data are collected at the establishment level on firm characteristics and on a sample of jobs within each firm. By contrast, the CPS is a monthly questionnaire administered to more than 60,000 households, with questions pertaining to employment status, occupation, wages, and hours worked, among other subjects.[48]

The NCS has been used recently by some analysts (most prominently by Podgursky 2003 and Vedder 2003) to compare the wages of teachers with those of other professionals. In particular, these analyses have used the NCS to compare *hourly* wages across occupations—a sensible approach, given the shorter "official" work year (and arguably shorter work week) of teachers.[49] Data on hourly pay, in this light, could potentially allow an analysis to avoid the problem of differing work schedules across occupations. These analysts' finding that teachers earn more per hour than lawyers, computer programmers, and other professionals, however, did not match our priors (our intuition and sense of the world), nor our sense of the previous literature on relative teacher pay (Chapter I). Thus, we sought to gain a better understanding of the differences between the NCS and CPS in the measurement of weekly wages, hours, and hourly wages. It should be noted that the NCS data have only recently become available; consequently, NCS methodologies and peculiarities are not well known in the research community. As we show below, vast differences in the way work time is measured in the NCS for

**Table 10  Mean wages and hours worked by elementary and secondary teachers, in the 2002 NCS and CPS**

|  | NCS | CPS | Difference | % Difference |
|---|---|---|---|---|
| Elementary teachers: |  |  |  |  |
| Mean weekly wage | $1,123 | $846 | $277 | 32.7% |
| Mean weekly hours | 36.4 | 43.5 | -7.1 | -16.3 |
| Mean hourly wage | $30.80 | $19.90 | $10.90 | 54.8 |
| Secondary teachers: |  |  |  |  |
| Mean weekly wage | $1,147 | $896 | $251 | 28.0% |
| Mean weekly hours | 37.0 | 43.9 | -6.9 | -15.7 |
| Mean hourly wage | $31.00 | $21.20 | $9.80 | 46.2 |

Source: Authors' analysis.

teachers (K-12, as well as university professors) and workers following a more traditional year-round schedule preclude an accurate comparison of relative hourly pay in the NCS.

In **Table 10**, we compute the mean weekly wage, hours worked per week, and hourly wage for elementary and secondary school teachers, using data from the CPS-ORG and NCS.[50] In contrast to the CPS, the NCS has much *higher* weekly wages (32.7% higher for elementary teachers; 28.0% higher for secondary teachers) and much *lower* weekly hours (roughly seven fewer hours for each group; a 16% difference). Taken together, these large differences in weekly wages and weekly hours worked produce even greater differences in hourly wages, with the NCS suggesting nearly 50% greater earnings per hour.

Differences between the NCS and CPS in the measurement of weekly wages and hours worked will affect measures of relative pay only to the extent that these differences vary across occupations. **Figures 5** and **6** examine the differences between the NCS and the CPS for mean weekly wages and hours worked for *all* occupations, sorted in descending order by the percentage difference between NCS and CPS; selected teaching occupations are highlighted (a positive percentage difference in these figures indicates that the NCS mean exceeds that found in the CPS; the closer the difference is to zero, the less the discrepancy between the two surveys).

Figure 5 shows the percentage difference between the NCS and the CPS for mean weekly wages, by occupation. The differences are about evenly distributed—with about half positive and half negative. This figure suggests that the NCS overstates average weekly wages for roughly half of all occupations, and understates them for the other half (relative to the CPS). However, 44% of the occupations that are at or above the 90th percentile of differences are teaching occupations (including university professors); these occupations account for 58%

**Figure 5  Percent difference between NCS and ORG average weekly wages, by occupation**

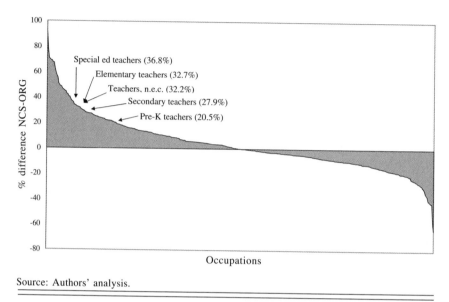

Source: Authors' analysis.

**Figure 6  Percent difference between NCS and ORG average hours per week, by occupation**

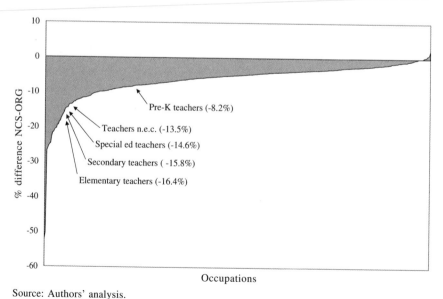

Source: Authors' analysis.

## Figure 7  Percent difference between NCS and ORG average hourly wages, by occupation

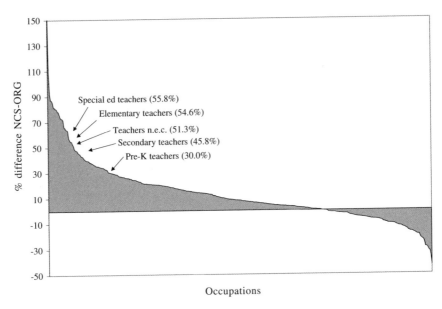

Source: Authors' analysis.

of all teachers in the distribution. It appears that the wages of teaching occupations are much more likely to be overstated in the NCS (relative to the CPS), and to a greater extent, than are most other professions.

Figure 6 shows the discrepancies between the NCS and CPS for mean weekly hours worked, by occupation. The most striking feature of this figure is that, for almost all occupations (97% of them, in fact), NCS weekly hours are *less* than those of the CPS. Only 3% of all occupations have greater work hours reported in the NCS than in the CPS. In general, NCS data on average hours worked per week are understated for nearly all occupations (compared to the CPS). As with Figure 5, teaching occupations are concentrated among the greatest NCS-CPS discrepancies, where the NCS greatly *understates* average hours worked per week, relative to the CPS. Again, 49% of teaching occupations are below the bottom 10th percentile of differences, representing nearly 65% of all teaching professions.

As might be expected, NCS-CPS discrepancies are compounded when weekly wages and weekly hours worked are combined to compute hourly wages; these percent differences are displayed in **Figure 7**. The differences in average hourly wages are much larger than when average weekly wages are compared. Forty-eight percent of occupations at the 90th percentile and above are teaching occupations, and they account for 65% of all teachers.

The analysis above suggests that the pattern of weekly wages, weekly hours, and hourly wages for teaching occupations is far different in the NCS than in the CPS. The differences between the NCS and the CPS for most professional occupations are not nearly as large. This may explain why a comparison of hourly wages between teachers and other professionals using the NCS produces somewhat non-intuitive results.

We investigated further the measurement of wages and work time in the NCS and found that the measurement of work time for teachers is inconsistent with that of other workers and professionals. In fact, this different treatment of work time in the NCS appears to apply to nearly all occupations that do not have regular year-round schedules, and it accounts for nearly all of the discrepancy between the NCS and CPS measures of weekly and hourly wages.

When comparing mean *annual* wages of elementary and secondary teachers in the NCS with those from various other surveys (the BLS Occupational Employment Survey, the Department of Education Schools and Staffing Survey, and the American Federation of Teachers and National Education Association surveys of state education departments), they appear similar. Thus, it did not seem likely to us that the NCS measure of annual wages was responsible for the NCS-CPS discrepancy.

We next compared mean weeks and hours worked for K-12 teaching occupations with those of private sector professionals (excluding most teachers) and for selected other professional occupations in the NCS. The data in **Table 11** suggest that weeks worked are measured differently in the NCS for teachers than for other professional occupations. Teachers are considered to have worked an average of 38 weeks in 2001, while other professionals worked an average of 51-52 weeks. A 38-week working year (as is the case for teachers) implies nine months of work, or a 190-day work year (apparently excluding summers off, and any paid holidays or vacations). Thus, the measurement of weeks for teachers clearly corresponds to actual "weeks worked" rather than "weeks paid." In contrast, data collected on professionals appear to be on a "weeks paid" basis. Here, the 52-week working year clearly *does include* federal holidays and vacation time.

This inconsistency in the measurement of weeks worked creates a substantial bias in relative weekly wages. If we assume, very conservatively, that non-teaching professionals actually work 48 weeks per year (i.e., have 20 days of paid leave) rather than 52, then non-teaching weekly wages must be adjusted upward by 8.3%.[51]

Given these inconsistencies, it is not surprising that the BLS chief of the Division of Compensation Data Estimation National Compensation Survey noted, in correspondence:

> The futility of comparing salary estimates for periods of less than a year between two occupations with very dissimilar work time requirements over the year and for whom the annual leave entitlements are unknown.
> ...Because the published NCS wage estimates do not reflect leave entitle-

**Table 11 Annual and weekly hours and weeks worked by full-time workers, in the NCS, by occupation, 2001**

|                                | Annual hours | Weekly hours | Weeks |
|--------------------------------|:------------:|:------------:|:-----:|
| Elementary teachers            | 1,390        | 36.5         | 38.1  |
| Secondary teachers             | 1,417        | 37.1         | 38.2  |
| Professionals, private sector  | 2,024        | 39.7         | 51.0  |
| Engineers, architects, surveyors | 2,114      | 40.7         | 51.9  |
| Editors and reporters          | 2,050        | 39.5         | 51.9  |
| Computer programmers           | 2,058        | 39.6         | 52.0  |
| Accountants and auditors       | 2,041        | 39.6         | 51.5  |
| Lawyers                        | 2,056        | 39.5         | 52.1  |

Source: Authors' analysis.

ments and the work years of teachers are so dissimilar from most other professional occupations, I would only use the annual salary estimates from NCS to compare teacher pay with the pay of other professionals.[52]

There are also inconsistencies in how weekly work hours are measured for teachers and for other professions in the NCS. Teachers' mean weekly hours are 36.4 for elementary and 37.0 for secondary teachers in the NCS (Table 10); these weekly hours are computed as contracted hours of work each day, less the time for lunch and other breaks, multiplied by the number of working days per week. In contrast, teachers report an average of 43.9 weekly hours in the CPS, roughly seven hours, or 20%, more per week than in the NCS. Non-teaching professionals' hours reported corresponded more closely to the traditional 40-hour week. While non-teaching professionals' hours are understated (relative to that reported in the CPS), teachers' weekly hours appeared much *more* likely to be understated, and to a greater degree, than those of the typical professional worker.

Hours reported by teachers in the CPS are consistent with other data that suggest teachers work 1.5 hours per workday beyond the official scheduled work time. A teacher's official on-site work hours are determined at the school or district level, usually through the collective bargaining agreement; these agreements are specific about the length of the working day, as well as time allocated per day for lunch and planning periods.[53] In practice, however, the typical teacher spends a good deal more time devoted to teaching responsibilities than that specified by the collective bargaining agreement. Since these agreements do not explicitly address hours worked outside of the contracted school day, researchers have been forced to look elsewhere for evidence on time devoted to the teaching profession. Drago et al. (1999), for instance, conducted a time diary survey of elementary

**Table 12 Time diary estimates of 1998 elementary school teacher work hours**

| | Hours per day of: | | | |
|---|---|---|---|---|
| | Contract time | "Site" time | Standard diary time | Work invasiveness |
| Entire sample | 6.50 | 8.26 | 9.69 | 10.28 |
| Men only | | 8.22 | 10.12 | 10.70 |
| Women only | | 8.26 | 9.63 | 10.22 |
| By age | | | | |
| 23-30 | | 8.32 | 9.63 | 10.13 |
| 31-40 | | 8.18 | 9.30 | 9.80 |
| 41-50 | | 8.17 | 9.48 | 10.21 |
| 51 and older | | 8.40 | 10.32 | 10.89 |

Source: Drago et al. (1999). "Site time" refers to time physically spent in the workplace; standard diary time includes site time plus time spent working at home (leisure time at home and work are excluded); "work invasiveness" includes all time devoted to work, at any time, any place (includes phone calls, emails, etc.).

school teachers in Wisconsin to determine how much time teachers spend working outside of their contract. Their results are summarized in **Table 12**. While the average elementary teacher in their sample was contracted to work 6.5 hours per day, or 32.5 hours per week, this teacher spent an average of 8.3 hours per day at the workplace ("site time") and 9.7 total hours per day devoted to work (both at school and at home).[54]

These time diary estimates in Wisconsin do not appear out of line with recent nationwide estimates of teacher work hours. **Table 13** presents mean weekly hours of work time, both during and outside school hours, for elementary, secondary, and all teachers from the Schools and Staffing Survey Teacher Questionnaires (SASS). The SASS distinguishes between hours spent outside of school working with students (together with required work hours, likely equivalent to Drago et al.'s "site time" measure) and hours outside of school working on other activities (planning, grading, etc).[55] In the 1999-2000 year, the average teacher was required to be in school 37.9 hours per week (about 7.5 per day, a bit higher than that in the Wisconsin time diary study), but spent an additional 11.9 hours per week before and after school on work-related activities (or 2.4 per day; this figure was lower for elementary teachers, at 2.1 per day). The 1999-2000 estimate of 8.2 daily hours of "face time" (hours required to be in school plus time spent with students outside of the school day) for all teachers is nearly the same as the 8.3 estimate in Drago et al. (1999). There is some evidence that both contracted work hours and time spent working outside of school hours have risen over time. In the 1990-91 version of the SASS, the average teacher was required to be in school 35.3 hours per week and spent 7.9 hours per week in grading and planning activities; as mentioned above, the averages in 1999-2000 were 37.9 and 8.7, respectively.[56]

In sum, teachers' hours per week reported in the National Compensation Survey (36.5 for elementary, 37.1 for secondary; Table 9) appear to correspond closely to contracted hours, or hours required to be in school in the SASS (37.6 for elementary, 38.2 for secondary); the higher number of hours per week reported in the CPS (43.5 and 43.9) are closer to that reported by teachers in time diary studies and on the SASS Teacher Questionnaire (48.4 and 51.4). In fact, weekly hours reported in the CPS still appear to underestimate actual hours devoted to school activities by almost five hours per week. At the very least, hours worked per week as reported in the CPS appear to be a lower bound to the number of hours teachers actually commit to their work each week.

How important are these discrepancies in measurement of weekly work hours for the relative hourly wage? If we assume that the 6.5% gap between CPS and NCS hours for professional occupations represents the "typical" reporting difference between the CPS and the NCS (that is, not specific to any occupation), then the remaining hours gap for teachers can be thought of as a necessary adjustment to teacher hours in the NCS. Applying the 6.5% gap to the mean weekly hours of teachers increases working hours from 36.6 to 38.9. The remaining gap between those 38.9 hours and the 43.9 hours in the CPS is a 4.9-hour or 12.9% gap. Thus, even allowing for a "normal" 6.5% hours difference between the NCS and CPS, teacher hours are still understated in the NCS by 12.9%.

Taken together, the inconsistencies in measurement of annual weeks and weekly hours worked between teaching and non-teaching occupations creates substantially biased estimates of the relative hourly wage of teachers. If we believe that the non-teaching weekly wage needs to be raised by 8.3% (to allow for 20 days paid leave for other professionals) and that teachers' hours are understated by 12.9%, then inconsistencies in measurement in the NCS obscure the fact that other professionals earn hourly wages 23.4% greater than do teachers.[57]

The NCS is a new survey and still developing. Correspondence from BLS notes:

> We are actively studying which occupations and groups of occupations should not have earnings estimated and published by hour. Flight crews on airlines, outside sales representatives, operating personnel on over-the-road railroads are but a few of the occupations in addition to teachers. The point of this research is to define comprehensive requirements for the estimation systems changes contemplated for 2007. While we cannot change the tables before 2007, we may be able to amend the introduction sections to our local and national bulletins to include a cautionary note in the near future.[58]

**Table 13 Reported hours of work—all teachers, elementary, and secondary teachers**

| | 1987-88 | 1990-91 | 1993-94 | 1999-2000 | 1999-2000 (per day) |
|---|---|---|---|---|---|
| **All public teachers:** | | | | | |
| Hours required to be in school | | 35.3 | | 37.9 | 7.57 |
| Hours of before-school, after-school, and weekend interaction with students | 2.6 | 3.1 | | 3.2 | 0.64 |
| Hours of before-school, after-school, and weekend planning and grading | 6.8 | 7.9 | | 8.7 | 1.75 |
| Total hours of school-related activities | | 46.3 | | 49.8 | 9.96 |
| **Elementary teachers:** | | | | | |
| Hours required to be in school | | | 33.0 | 37.6 | 7.51 |
| Hours of before-school, after-school, and weekend interaction with students | | | 1.7 | 1.7 | 0.35 |
| Hours of before-school, after-school, and weekend planning and grading | | | 9.2 | 9.1 | 1.82 |
| Total hours of school-related activities | | | 44.0 | 48.4 | 9.67 |
| **Secondary teachers:** | | | | | |
| Hours required to be in school | | | 33.3 | 38.2 | 7.64 |
| Hours of before-school, after-school, and weekend interaction with students | | | 4.9 | 4.8 | 0.97 |
| Hours of before-school, after-school, and weekend planning and grading | | | 8.2 | 8.3 | 1.67 |
| Total hours of school-related activities | | | 46.5 | 51.4 | 10.27 |

Source: Authors' analysis of SASS Teacher Questionnaires.

Our conclusion is that hourly or weekly wage data from the NCS (as given) should not be used to make comparisons between teachers and other occupations; we therefore rely on weekly wages from the CPS-ORG in our analysis in Chapter II of this report.

# CONCLUSION

Our empirical foray into estimating teacher relative wages provides some advances over the prior literature. For some reason, analysts have failed to use the CPS-ORG data on weekly wages to estimate teacher relative wages, even though this is one of the most heavily used data sets for analyzing wages. Using the ORG, however, requires overcoming the challenge of the bias imparted by the imputation process and a discontinuity in the series due to the CPS redesign. Despite these challenges, we think these are valuable, if not the most valuable, data for these purposes. We also innovated by using the NCS occupational leveling factor criteria, or measurement of skills, to systematically identify occupations that are comparable to teachers. This grouping of 16, or the eight largest occupations, holds promise for use in other empirical settings. Our examination of the fringe benefit bias helps to clarify the discussion of teacher pay by quantifying the effect of teachers having a somewhat better benefit package (assuming a CPS-type W-2 wage measure) on the assessment of teacher relative wages or pay. All in all, incorporating benefits into the analysis does not alter the general picture of teachers having a substantial wage/pay disadvantage that eroded considerably over the last 10 years. Last, our examination of the underlying methodology of the NCS yielded an important insight into the uses and limitations of the NCS data. One limitation is that it is not appropriate to compare weekly or hourly wages of occupations that are part-year or have irregular work hours to other occupations that conform to a more usual 52-week, 40-hours-per-week schedule.

Our findings should inform policy makers that the recent erosion of teacher relative pay will make sustaining and improving teacher quality harder in the future. The results do not directly address difficulties in recruiting teachers in particular locations, such as rural schools or inner-city hard-to-staff schools, or in particular subject areas. Some of this we intend to explore in further work.

**Appendix Table A  Weekly wages of teachers, non-teacher college graduates, and all workers 1983-2003**

| Year | Pooled | | | Female college graduates | | Male college graduates | |
|---|---|---|---|---|---|---|---|
| | All workers | College graduates | Teachers | Not teachers | Teachers | Not teachers | Teachers |
| 1983 | $602 | $816 | $654 | $648 | $630 | $942 | $720 |
| 1984 | 605 | 823 | 683 | 661 | 653 | 946 | 759 |
| 1985 | 611 | 835 | 694 | 677 | 668 | 957 | 769 |
| 1986 | 633 | 888 | 728 | 708 | 700 | 1027 | 815 |
| 1987 | 634 | 895 | 742 | 724 | 714 | 1030 | 830 |
| 1988 | 631 | 892 | 743 | 722 | 714 | 1027 | 827 |
| 1989 | 649 | 926 | 747 | 750 | 725 | 1074 | 814 |
| 1990 | 649 | 929 | 761 | 759 | 742 | 1074 | 826 |
| 1991 | 649 | 925 | 759 | 766 | 738 | 1067 | 835 |
| 1992 | 652 | 933 | 769 | 783 | 749 | 1069 | 840 |
| 1993 | 656 | 936 | 775 | 793 | 759 | 1069 | 843 |
| **(CPS redesign\*)** | | | | | | | |
| 1994 | | | | | | | |
| 1995 | 682 | 968 | 839 | 822 | 821 | 1093 | 911 |
| 1996 | 682 | 965 | 826 | 828 | 809 | 1094 | 902 |
| 1997 | 685 | 967 | 812 | 834 | 801 | 1097 | 876 |
| 1998 | 710 | 1018 | 821 | 866 | 816 | 1169 | 872 |
| 1999 | 737 | 1055 | 833 | 895 | 827 | 1238 | 889 |
| 2000 | 747 | 1073 | 827 | 918 | 818 | 1251 | 891 |
| 2001 | 758 | 107a9 | 825 | 922 | 828 | 1251 | 862 |
| 2002 | 760 | 1074 | 818 | 924 | 813 | 1245 | 876 |
| 2003 | 766 | 1078 | 833 | 933 | 820 | 1246 | 899 |
| 1983-89 | 8.0% | 13.5% | 14.3% | 15.8% | 15.2% | 14.0% | 13.1% |
| 1989-93 | 1.0 | 1.1 | 3.6 | 5.7 | 4.7 | -0.5 | 3.6 |
| 1996-2003 | 12.3 | 11.8 | 0.8 | 12.7 | 1.3 | 13.9 | -0.3 |

\* The redesign of the CPS boosted teacher wages relative to other wages, thereby making the data before and after 1994 not comparable.

Source: Authors' analysis.

**Appendix Table B Ratio of teacher weekly wages to other college graduates by gender, 1983-2003**

| Year | Pooled Teachers to: | | Female Teachers to: | Male Teachers to: |
|------|-------|----------|----------|----------|
| | All | College graduates | College graduates | College graduates |
| 1983 | 1.087 | 0.802 | 0.972 | 0.764 |
| 1984 | 1.130 | 0.830 | 0.989 | 0.803 |
| 1985 | 1.136 | 0.831 | 0.987 | 0.803 |
| 1986 | 1.151 | 0.820 | 0.989 | 0.794 |
| 1987 | 1.171 | 0.829 | 0.986 | 0.806 |
| 1988 | 1.177 | 0.833 | 0.989 | 0.805 |
| 1989 | 1.151 | 0.807 | 0.967 | 0.758 |
| 1990 | 1.173 | 0.820 | 0.978 | 0.769 |
| 1991 | 1.169 | 0.821 | 0.963 | 0.783 |
| 1992 | 1.179 | 0.824 | 0.956 | 0.786 |
| 1993 | 1.181 | 0.828 | 0.958 | 0.789 |
| 1995 | 1.230 | 0.867 | 0.998 | 0.833 |
| 1996 | 1.210 | 0.856 | 0.977 | 0.824 |
| 1997 | 1.185 | 0.840 | 0.961 | 0.799 |
| 1998 | 1.156 | 0.807 | 0.942 | 0.746 |
| 1999 | 1.131 | 0.790 | 0.923 | 0.730 |
| 2000 | 1.108 | 0.771 | 0.891 | 0.720 |
| 2001 | 1.089 | 0.765 | 0.898 | 0.689 |
| 2002 | 1.077 | 0.762 | 0.880 | 0.704 |
| 2003 | 1.087 | 0.772 | 0.879 | 0.721 |
| **Change in wage ratios** | | | | |
| 1983-89 | 0.06 | 0.006 | -0.005 | -0.006 |
| 1989-93 | 0.03 | 0.020 | -0.009 | 0.031 |
| 1996-2003 | -0.12 | -0.084 | -0.099 | -0.103 |

Source: Authors' analysis.

## Appendix Table C  Estimated teacher relative weekly wage*

|  | Pooled | Women | Men |
|---|---|---|---|
| 1979 | -6.8% | 2.9% | -22.1% |
| 1980 | -9.2 | 0.8 | -24.1 |
| 1981 | -9.1 | -1.0 | -22.0 |
| 1982 | -9.2 | -0.7 | -21.8 |
| 1983 | -10.3 | -2.1 | -22.0 |
| 1984 | -8.1 | -0.4 | -20.1 |
| 1985 | -8.2 | -1.2 | -19.9 |
| 1986 | -8.1 | -0.6 | -19.7 |
| 1987 | -7.3 | -0.1 | -19.3 |
| 1988 | -7.5 | 0.0 | -18.9 |
| 1989 | -9.2 | -1.4 | -21.6 |
| 1990 | -8.7 | -0.6 | -21.5 |
| 1991 | -9.8 | -2.8 | -20.2 |
| 1992 | -8.9 | -2.1 | -20.1 |
| 1993 | -8.5 | -2.6 | -18.9 |
| 1994** |  |  |  |
| 1995** |  |  |  |
| 1996 | -6.6 | -2.6 | -16.9 |
| 1997 | -7.4 | -2.9 | -18.9 |
| 1998 | -10.6 | -5.1 | -22.6 |
| 1999 | -11.3 | -5.6 | -22.9 |
| 2000 | -12.9 | -8.5 | -23.2 |
| 2001 | -14.1 | -8.1 | -26.0 |
| 2002 | -15.0 | -10.0 | -25.7 |
| 2003 | -13.6 | -8.9 | -23.1 |
| 1979-93 | -1.7% | -5.5% | 3.2% |
| 1996-2003 | -7.0 | -6.3 | -6.2 |

\* Teachers weekly wage relative to other workers controlling for education, age as a quartic, region, marital status, and race/ethnicity.

\*\* Data for 1994 and 1995 not available because imputed wages cannot be identified.

Source: Authors' analysis.

# Endnotes

1. See Hanushek (1971), Ehrenberg and Brewer (1995), Ferguson and Ladd (1996), Hanushek, Kain, and Rivkin (1998), and Rockoff (2004) for examples. Rice (2003) provides a review of the literature.

2. Corcoran, Evans, and Schwab (2004) and Murnane et al. (1991).

3. See Jepsen and Rivkin (2004) for evidence on how small class size initiatives in California have complicated the task of recruiting high-quality teachers in that state.

4. Weaver (1983) recounts a long history of public debate over teacher pay and teacher quality.

5. See Podgursky (2003) and Vedder (2003), for example.

6. This does not mean that the NCS is not useful for other purposes. The problem is comparing the hourly or weekly wages of occupations when not all maintain regular year-round, full-time work schedules.

7. Nelson and Drown (2003), Table II-1. The American Federation of Teachers (AFT) has used its annual survey of state education departments to estimate average teacher salaries since 1977-78. Prior to this year, salaries were taken from the *Digest of Education Statistics* (which in turn obtains salaries from the National Education Association, *Estimates of School Statistics*). Average K-12 annual teaching salaries in the 2002 *Digest* are consistent with those of the AFT ($30,292 in 1959-60 and $44,604 in 2001-02.)

8. We address this below in Chapter II.

9. Recent examples of this type of analysis can be found in Nelson and Drown (2003), Goldhaber (2001), Vedder (2003), Podgursky (2003), Temin (2002), Ballou and Podgursky (1997), and Hanushek and Rivkin (1997, 2004). Some of these studies alternatively provide the rank of the wage of the average teacher in the comparison group's wage distribution.

10. Hanushek and Rivkin (2004) and Bacolod (2003).

11. Ballou and Podgursky (1997) obtain the same result for new (first-year) teachers using data from the Department of Education's Recent College Graduates survey over the 1979 to 1989 period.

12.   Nelson and Drown (2003). Gains in the 1970s and 1980s were likely due to changes in the gender composition of these comparable professions.

13.   This finding—that teacher pay gained relative to that of other professions—is likely due to the differential change in demographics between teachers and these other professions, as discussed above.

14.   Ballou and Podgursky propose two explanations for this lack of responsiveness to salary: (1) increases in teacher pay between 1979 and 1989 were targeted at *all* teachers rather than new teachers, effectively lowering quit rates among existing teachers and reducing job opportunities for new teachers, and (2) increases in teacher pay increased the pool of applicants but public schools did not appear to have a preference for the strongest candidates (see Ballou 1996 and Manksi 1985). It has been argued elsewhere (see Corcoran, Evans, and Schwab 2004) that standardized test scores of prospective, rather than actual, education majors (like those used in Ballou and Podgursky 1997) are likely a noisy measure of the relative quality of practicing teachers, particularly when comparisons are being made across time.

15.   Corcoran, Evans, and Schwab (2004), Murnane et al. (1991), and Bacolod (2003).

16.   Hoxby and Leigh (2004) provide an alternative view, in which they suggest that wage compression brought about by increased unionization of the teaching profession has led to a decline in the fraction of top graduates choosing the teaching profession.

17.   Hanushek (1986, 1997), Betts (1995), Grogger (1996).

18.   In other words, all else equal, teacher pay (as well as that in other professions) will be less in those school districts that are the most desirable places to live, based on characteristics such as weather or natural beauty. If student outcomes are correlated with these district characteristics, a cross-sectional study of teacher pay and student outcomes is likely to find no correlation (or even a negative correlation) between teacher pay and student performance. For this reason, Stoddard (2003) does not recommend adjusting salaries for the "cost of living," as rents and wages adjust to reflect local amenities.

19.   Some of our data are presented only back to 1983. We will extend it to 1979 in further work. The trend in relative hourly wages is nearly identical to that for weekly wages; we therefore include only our analysis of weekly wages. Results for hourly wages are available upon request.

20.   The CPS-ORG provides a more accurate measure of weekly earnings than the March CPS, since respondents are asked specifically about the most recent week of work. In the March CPS, weekly earnings are calculated using annual wages and weeks worked in the prior year.

21. Full time refers to hours greater than or equal to 35 in the ORG data wages.

22. See Podgursky (2003) and Vedder (2003).

23. In ongoing work we are attempting to estimate teachers' relative annual wages and adjust these estimates for lost earnings and gained leisure opportunities in the summer.

24. In 1995 it is possible to identify observations with imputed data for the last four months, but that is insufficient data for charting trends.

25. The bump up from the redesign may be due to the following: before 1994, some teachers may have been reporting weekly wages equivalent to their part-year salary spread over 52 weeks, but after 1994 they were able to report an annual salary, which was then allocated to the actual number of weeks worked. This implies that teacher weekly wages in the CPS were artificially low before 1994. That is why we focus on estimates of the cross-section teacher relative wage only for recent years. We have no reason to believe that the extent to which the CPS understated teacher weekly wages changed over the 1979-93 (pre-redesign) period. Thus, we examine separately the 1979-93 and post-1994 periods.

26. Note that the column for teachers includes all teachers, not just those with college degrees. The movement of wages of all teachers and those with college degrees, however, is identical over the 1983-2003 period among women, suggesting no bias from including or excluding the small number of teachers without college degrees.

27. We employ a standard model with the log of weekly wages as the dependent variable with a dummy variable for teachers as our main explanatory variable. Additionally, controls for education (four education dummy variables), age as a quartic, marital status, region, and race/ethnicity are included. The coefficient on the dummy variable for those who are teachers provides the estimate of teacher relative wages (how much teachers earn relative to comparable workers) controlling for other worker characteristics. (We present the exponentiated value of the coefficient less 1.) This analysis assumes teachers and other college graduates have the same returns to education and experience, an assumption we relax in other estimations reported below.

28. The redesign problem means we cannot identify a change in the relative wages between 1993 and 1994. The inability to identify imputed observations means we cannot identify changes in relative wages for 1993-94, 1994-95, and 1995-96.

29. See Flyer and Rosen (1997) for more details. Regressions included controls for race, education level, and a quartic in age.

30. This is discussed in greater detail in Allegretto, Corcoran, and Mishel (2004).

31.   In particular, we ran regressions that had a control for union coverage.

32.   Younger teachers, however, have wages further behind comparable college graduates than do their older teacher colleagues.

33.   For example, the AFT in its annual survey of salaries compares teacher salaries to those of accountants, buyers, attorneys, computer systems analysts, engineers, and university professors.

34.   Podgursky (2003) questions the AFT's choice of comparable occupations, asking "where, one wonders, are the comparisons with journalists, registered nurses, district attorneys, FBI agents, military officers, and other not-so-highly compensated professionals and public-sector employees?" Podgursky presents occupational comparisons but does not elaborate on his selection criteria.

35.   In this analysis of comparable occupations our definition of K-12 teachers includes "special education" teachers, occupation code #158, as well as elementary and secondary teachers. The addition of special education teachers in this analysis does not affect the results materially and reflects a definition of teachers that we used in the first stages of our work.

36.   Pierce's regressions use the natural log of hourly wages as the dependent variable. In Chapter V, we argue that it is inappropriate to compare the hourly wages of teachers and non-teaching professionals using the NCS. Thus, Pierce's regression estimates are only valid here to the extent that they are unaffected (or affected little) by the presence of teachers (and other intermittent workers) in his sample. It seems likely that teachers and similar professions should make up a relatively small fraction of Pierce's sample of jobs.

37.   More details on the selection procedure are provided in Allegretto, Corcoran, and Mishel (2004).

38.   We calculate these averages using only the non-imputed CPS-ORG observations.

39.   We use only observations with non-imputed wage data for this comparison. Again, the weekly hours are what household respondents provide and are not "site-based" or contractual hours.

40.   Averages based on weekly wage data from the CPS-ORG, using non-imputed observations only.

41.   Podgursky (2003, 73-74), for instance, introduces his discussion of fringe benefits by saying "Neither AFT nor the NEA makes any adjustments for the fringe benefits associated with teaching in a public school, thus masking an important part of total compensation."

42. If the teacher advantage is less for benefits than wages, as per Vedder's example, then the teacher advantage for compensation would be *less* than for wages. Vedder generates the opposite result when he adds the two premiums. The teacher advantage (or disadvantage) for compensation is simply a weighted average of the advantage (disadvantage) for wages and for benefits, with the weights being the wage and benefit shares of total compensation.

43. See U.S. Department of Labor (2000, 2004c). Unfortunately, there are no detailed teacher compensation data available from the ECEC series for years before 1994.

44. Compare for instance the benefit share of compensation for a worker with $10,000 of benefits annually and a nine-month salary of $60,000 with a year-round worker with the same annual benefits and a salary of $80,000 (which is the same salary per month as the part-year worker).

45. Teachers are also more likely to have defined benefit pensions, which are superior to the defined contribution plans provided to many professionals (a superiority derived because workers bear the risks rather than employers with a defined contribution plan). Our analysis focuses only on employer costs and does not take qualitative differences in benefits into account.

46. This corresponds to the teacher relative wage effect of 13.6% that we found in the regression analysis reported in Table 2.

47. Detailed information about the NCS can be obtained at the Bureau of Labor Statistics website: http://www.bls.gov/ncs/home.htm and in Department of Labor (2003, 2004b).

48. See Bureau of Labor Statistics (2002), Technical Paper 63RV, or the Current Population Survey website (http://www.bls.census.gov/cps/cpsmain.htm) for more information about the CPS. As in Chapter II, we use the CPS-ORG (not the March CPS) for weekly wages.

49. Again, some teachers think of themselves as full-year workers, with summers devoted to professional development and classroom preparation.

50. Only non-imputed observations have been used in the CPS-ORG.

51. If weekly wages are calculated as annual wages divided by 52 (using 52 weeks per year) rather than by 48 weeks, then the true weekly wage is 8.3% higher when expressed as wages per week worked. Professionals are usually provided with more than 20 days of paid leave. According to National Compensation Survey data on benefits, Department of Labor (2004d), white-collar workers with 15 years experience (for teachers' experience in 2002 see Nelson and Drown 2003, 28) have 18.8 days of vacation. White-collar workers are also provided, on average, eight paid holidays, so together with vacations they have a total of 26.8 days of paid leave. Workers in larger establishments (those with 100 or more workers)

have 19.9 vacation days and nine holidays for a total of 28.9 paid days off. If we use paid leave for workers in larger establishments as our standard, then to make other occupations in the NCS comparable to teachers we would need to raise the weekly wages of comparable occupations by 12.6%. This seems a conservative standard because professionals in large establishment would enjoy even greater paid leave than the average worker in these establishments.

52.   Email correspondence from Paul Scheible (Chief, Division of Compensation Data Estimation National Compensation Survey) on April 27, 2004.

53.   For example, the following passages are found in the Pittsburgh Federation of Teachers Local 400 collective bargaining agreement (Articles 46 and 47): "the total length of the workday for teachers at the elementary school level shall be six (6) hours and fifty-five (55) minutes, including the minimum of a forty-five (45) minute lunch period." "Teachers in secondary schools shall normally be scheduled to teach five (5) class periods per day...teaching periods shall be no more than forty-five (45) minutes in length" (see http://www.aft.org/research/models/contracts/teacher/pit/a45-50.htm#46).

54.   It is not clear whether or not these totals includes lunch; if not, assuming a 30- to 45-minute lunch period would bring this average into line with the above Pittsburgh example (7 hours per day) and slightly below the average reported in the NCS (7.3 hours per day for elementary teachers).

55.   Specifically, the 1999-2000 SASS asked: "(1) how many hours were you required to be at THIS school during your MOST RECENT FULL WEEK of teaching? (2a,b) during your MOST RECENT FULL WEEK of teaching, how many hours did you spend AFTER school, BEFORE school, and ON THE WEEKEND on each of the following types of activities? (a) school-related activities involving student interaction, such as coaching..., (b) other school-related activities, such as preparation, grading papers, parent...." Total hours is the sum of these three items.

56.   Work hour estimates from the SASS can be found in Perie, Baker, and Bobbitt (1997), Choy et al. (1993), and Henke et al. (1996).

57.   If one sets teacher and professional hourly wages to $30, the rate for secondary teachers, one can develop a weekly wage based on 37 and 40 hours for teachers and professionals, respectively. The annual wage is this weekly wage at 38.2 weeks for teachers and 52 weeks for professionals. "Corrected" hourly wages are developed by dividing the professional annual wage by 48 weeks and 40 hours and the teacher annual wage by 38.2 weeks and 41.7 hours (12.9% greater than the 38.2 hours). The resulting wage difference is 23.4%, $32.50 versus $26.33, where none existed at the beginning.

58.   Correspondence from Paul Scheible (Chief, Division of Compensation Data Estimation National Compensation Survey) on April 14, 2004.

# References

Allegretto, Sylvia, Sean Corcoran, and Lawrence Mishel. 2004. *Teacher Pay: Where Does it Stand?* Washington, D.C.: Economic Policy Institute.

Bacolod, Marigee. 2003. "Do Alternative Opportunities Matter? The Role of Female Labor Markets in the Decline of Teacher Quality, 1960-1990." Manuscript, University of California- Irvine, September.

Ballou, Dale.1996. "Do Public Schools Hire the Best Applicants?" *Quarterly Journal of Economics* 111(1): 97—134.

Ballou, Dale, and Michael Podgursky. 1997. *Teacher Pay and Teacher Quality.* Kalamazoo, Mich.: W.E. Upjohn Institute for Employment Research.

Betts, Julian. 1995. "Does School Quality Matter? Evidence From the National Longitudinal Survey of Youth." *Review of Economics and Statistics* 77: 231—247.

Chambers, Jay G. 1998. *Geographic Variations in Public Schools' Costs.* Washington, D.C.: U.S. Department of Education, National Center for Education Statistics. Publication 1998-04.

Choy, Susan P., et al. 1993. *America's Teachers: Profile of a Profession.* Washington, D.C.: U.S. Department of Education, National Center for Education Statistics. Publication 93-025.

Corcoran, Sean P., William N. Evans, and Robert S. Schwab. 2004. "Women, the Labor Market, and the Declining Relative Quality of Teachers." *Journal of Policy Analysis and Management.*

Current Population Survey. 2002. "Design and Methodology." Technical Paper 63RV. Washington, D.C.: Bureau of Labor Statistics.

Drago, Robert, et al. 1999. "New Estimates of Working Time for Elementary School Teachers." *Monthly Labor Review*, April, pp. 31—40.

Ehrenberg, Ronald G., and Dominic J. Brewer. 1995. "Did Teachers' Verbal Ability and Race Matter in the 1960s? Coleman Revisited." *Economics of Education Review* 21: 1—21.

Ferguson, Ronald F., and Helen F. Ladd. 1996. "How and Why Money Matters: An Analysis of Alabama Schools." In Helen F. Ladd, ed., *Holding Schools Accountable: Performance-Based Reform in Education.* Washington, D.C.: Brookings Institution.

Figlio, David. 1997. "Teachers' Salaries and Teacher Quality." *Economics Letters* 55: 267—271.

Figlio, David. 2002. "Can Public Schools Buy Better-Qualified Teachers?" *Industrial and Labor Relations Revew* 55(4): 686—699.

Flyer, Fredrick, and Sherwin Rosen. 1997. "The New Economics of Teachers and Education." *Journal of Labor Economics* 15(1): S104—139.

Goldhaber, Dan D. 2001. "How Has Teacher Compensation Changed?" *Selected Papers in School Finance, 2000-01*. Washington, D.C.: U.S. Department of Education, National Center for Education Statistics. Publication NCES 2001-378.

Grogger, Jeffrey. 1996. "School Expenditures and Post-Schooling Earnings: Evidence From High School and Beyond." *Review of Economics and Statistics* 78: 628—637.

Hanushek, Eric A. 1971. "Teacher Characteristics and Gains in Student Achievement." *American Economic Review* 61: 280—288.

Hanushek, Eric A. 1986. "The Economics of Schooling: Production and Efficiency in Public Schools." *Journal of Economic Literature* 24: 1141—1147.

Hanushek, Eric A. 1997. "Assessing the Effects of School Resources on Student Performance: An Update." *Educational Evaluation and Policy Analysis* 19: 141—164.

Hanushek, Eric A., John F. Kain, and Steven G. Rivkin. 1998. "Teachers, Schools, and Academic Achievement." Working Paper No. 6691. Cambridge, Mass.: National Bureau of Economic Research.

Hanushek, Eric A., John F. Kain, and Steven G. Rivkin. 1999. "Do Higher Salaries Buy Better Teachers?" Working Paper No. 7082. Cambridge, Mass.: National Bureau of Economic Research.

Hanushek, Eric A., and Steven G. Rivkin. 1997. "Understanding the Twentieth-Century Growth in U.S. School Spending." *Journal of Human Resources* 32(1): 35—68.

Hanushek, Eric A., and Steven G. Rivkin. 2004. "How to Improve the Supply of High-Quality Teachers." In Diane Ravitch, ed., *Brookings Papers on Education Policy 2004*. Washington, D.C.: Brookings Institution Press, pp. 7—25.

Henke, R.R., S. Geis, and J. Giambattista. 1996. *Out of the Lecture Hall and Into the Classroom: 1992-93 College Graduates and Elementary/Secondary School Teaching* (NCES 96-899). Washington, DC: National Center for Education Statistics, U.S. Department of Education.

Hirsch, Barry T., and Edward J. Schumacher. 2004 (forthcoming). "Match Bias in Wage Gap Estimates Due to Earnings Imputation." *Journal of Labor Economics* 22(3).

Hoxby, Caroline, and Andrew Leigh. 2004. "Pulled Away or Pushed Out? Explaining the Decline in Teacher Aptitude in the United States." *American Economic Review* 94(2): 236—240.

Jepsen, Christopher, and Steven Rivkin. 2004. "What Is the Tradeoff Between Smaller Classes and Teacher Quality?" Mimeo.

Lakdawalla, Darius. 2001. "Quantity Over Quality." *Education Next.* Fall.

Lakdawalla, Darius. 2002. "The Declining Relative Quality of Teachers. Working Paper No. 8263. Cambridge, Mass.: National Bureau of Economic Research.

Lillard, Lee, James P. Smith, and Finis Welch. 1986. "What Do We Really Know About Wages? The Importance of Nonreporting and Cenus Imputations." *The Journal of Political Economy* 94(3, Part 1): 489—506.

Loeb, Susanna, and Marianne Page. 2000. "Examining the Link Between Teacher Wages and Student Outcomes: The Importance of Alternative Labor Market Opportunities and Non-Pecuniary Variation." *Review of Economics and Statistics* 82(3): 393—408.

Manski, Charles. 1985. "Academic Ability, Earnings, and the Decision to Become a Teacher: Evidence From the National Longitudinal Study of the High School Class of 1972." Working Paper No. 1539. Cambridge, Mass.: National Bureau of Economic Research.

Mishel, Lawrence, Jared Bernstein, and Heather Boushey. 2003. *The State of Working America, 2002/ 2003*. Economic Policy Institute Series. New York: Cornell University Press.

Murnane, R.J., J.D. Singer, J.B. Willett, J.J. Kemple, and R.J. Olsen. 1991. *Who Will Teach? Policies that Matter.* Cambridge, Mass.: Harvard University Press.

National Center for Education Statistics. 2003. *Digest of Education Statistics 2002*. NCES 2003-060. Washington, D.C.: U.S. Department of Education, Office of Educational Research and Improvement.

Nelson, F. Howard, and Rachel Drown. 2003. *Survey and Analysis of Teacher Salary Trends: 2002*. Washington, D.C.: American Federation of Teachers.

Perie, M., D. Baker, and S. Bobbitt. 1997. *Time Spent Teaching Core Academic Subjects in Elementary Schools: Comparisons Across Community, School, Teachers, and Student Characteristics*. Washington, D.C.: U.S. Department of Education, Office of Educational Research and Improvement, Educational Resources Information Center, National Center for Education Statistics.

Pierce, Brooks. 1999. "Using the National Compensation Survey to Predict Wage Rates." *Compensation and Working Conditions*. Washington, D.C.: Bureau of Labor Statistics.

Podgursky, Michael. 2003. "Fringe Benefits." *Education Next* 3(3): 71—76.

Polivka, Anne E., and Stephen M. Miller. 1995. "The CPS After the Redesign: Refocusing the Economic Lens." Washington, D.C.: Bureau of Labor Statistics. http://www.bls.gov/ore/pdf/ec950090.pdf.

Rice, Jennifer King. 2003. *Teacher Quality: Understanding the Effectiveness of Teacher Attributes*. Washington, D.C.: Economic Policy Institute.

Rockoff, Jonah E. 2004. "The Impact of Individual Teachers on Student Achievement: Evidence From Panel Data." *American Economic Review, Papers and Proceedings of the American Economic Association* 94(2): 247—252.

Stoddard, Christiana. 2003. "Adjusting Teacher Salaries for the Cost of Living: The Effect on Salary Comparisons and Policy Conclusions." Mimeo, Montana State University.

Temin, Peter. 2002. "Teacher Quality and the Future of America." *Eastern Economic Journal* 28(3): 285—300.

Temin, Peter. 2003. "Low Pay, Low Quality." *Education Next* 3(3): 8—13.

U.S. Department of Labor, Bureau of Labor Statistics. 2000. *Employer Costs for Employee Compensation, 1986-99*. Bulletin 2526. Washington, D.C.: Department of Labor, March.

U.S. Department of Labor, Bureau of Labor Statistics. 2002. Technical Paper 63RV. Washington, D.C.: Department of Labor. www.census.gov/prod/2002pubs/tp63rv.pdf.

U.S. Department of Labor, Bureau of Labor Statistics. 2003. *National Compensation Survey: Occupational Wages in the United States, July 2002*. Bulletin 2561. Washington, D.C.: Department of Labor, September 2003.

U.S. Department of Labor, Bureau of Labor Statistics. 2004a. "Technical Notes for 2002 OES Estimates." Washington, D.C.: Department of Labor. www.bls.gov/oes/2002/oes_tec.htm.

U.S. Department of Labor, Bureau of Labor Statistics. 2004b. "Earnings Data" and "Work Schedule." In *Data Collection Procedures Manual*. Washington, D.C.: Department of Labor.

U.S. Department of Labor, Bureau of Labor Statistics. 2004c. *Employer Costs for Employee Compensation Historical Listing, 2002-2003*. Washington, D.C.: Department of Labor, February 26.

U. S. Department of Labor, Bureau of Labor Statistics. 2004d. *National Compensation Survey: Employee Benefits in Private Industry in the United States, March 2003*. Summary 04-02. Washington, D.C.: Department of Labor, April.

Vedder, Richard. 2003. "Comparable Worth." *Education Next* 3(3): 14—19.

Weaver, Timothy. 1983. *America's Teacher Quality Problem: Alternatives for Reform*. New York, N.Y.: Praeger.

# Titles of particular interest to educators from the Economic Policy Institute

*Reports are available at the EPI website, www.epinet.org.*

**Class and Schools: Using Social, Economic, and Educational Reform to Close the Black–White Achievement Gap**
Richard Rothstein

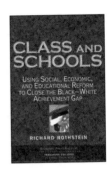

The wide and persistent achievement gap between black and white students is a key measure of the nation's failure to achieve true equality. As federal and state officials pursue tougher accountability and other reforms at the school level, they are neglecting an area that is vital to narrowing the achievement gap: social class differences that affect learning. *Class and Schools* — co-published by the Economic Policy Institute and Teachers College, Columbia University — shows that social class differences in health care quality and access, nutrition, childrearing styles, housing quality and stability, parental occupation and aspirations, and even exposure to environmental toxins play a significant part in how well children learn and ultimately succeed.

**Smart Money: Education and Economic Development**
William Schweke

Strong economies compete on the basis of high value, not solely low cost. The most forward-thinking approach to increasing U.S. competitiveness is to equip today's and tomorrow's citizens with the skills and attitudes needed for economic and civic success in an increasingly knowledge-based economy. *Smart Money* argues that funds spent on education pays off not only for workers, but for communities and businesses as well.

**Teacher Quality: Understanding the Effectiveness of Teacher Attributes**
Jennifer King Rice

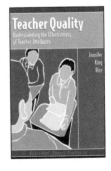

Teacher quality is the single most important school-related factor influencing student success. In this study Jennifer King Rice examines the body of research to draw conclusions about which attributes make teachers most effective, with a focus on aspects of teacher quality that can be translated into policy recommendations and incorporated into teaching practice.

## Inequality at the Starting Gate: Social Background Differences in Achievement as Children Begin School

Valerie E. Lee and David T. Burkam

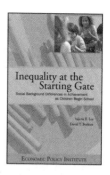

*Inequality at the Starting Gate* examines the learning gap between rich and poor children when they enter kindergarten. This study, by two education experts from the University of Michigan, analyzes U.S. Education Department data on 16,000 kindergartners nationwide, showing the direct link between student achievement gaps and socioeconomic status. The report finds that impoverished children lag behind their peers in reading and math skills even before they start school. The book also reveals how a lack of resources and opportunities can cause lasting academic damage to some children, underscoring the need for earlier and more comprehensive efforts to prepare children to succeed in school.

## Market-Based Reforms in Urban Education

Helen F. Ladd

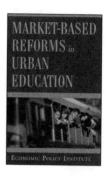

In the debate over reforming urban education, the issues surrounding market-based approaches — charter schools, vouchers, public school choice — are complex. This EPI book examines the extensive but disparate evidence to help determine whether these reforms promote the public interest and translate well into the provision of compulsory education.

## Where's the Payoff? The Gap Between Black Academic Progress and Economic Gains

Jared Bernstein

Blacks have made substantial progress toward closing educational gaps, yet their wages and employment opportunities continue to lag. A review of the evidence suggests that blacks are more likely than whites to be affected by adverse labor market trends, and they have the added burden of labor market discrimination.

## The Class Size Debate

Lawrence Mishel and Richard Rothstein, editors;
Alan B. Krueger, Eric A. Hanushek,
and Jennifer King Rice, contributors

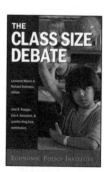

Two eminent economists — Professors Krueger and Hanushek — debate the merits of smaller class size and the research methods used to gauge the efficacy of this education reform measure. Professor Rice synthesizes their arguments and highlights the points of agreement in their different perspectives.

## School Choice: Examining the Evidence

Edith Rasell & Richard Rothstein, editors

Opinions about school choice have been formed largely on the basis of theoretical assertions that it offers the answer for the problems of public education. But researchers studying actual programs find that choice of schools neither raises student achievement nor enhances equality of opportunity, and may exacerbate racial segregation and socioeconomic stratification.

## Where's the Money Going? Changes in the
## Level and Composition of Education Spending, 1991-96
Richard Rothstein
A detailed analysis of spending by representative school districts shows that real per pupil spending in the U.S. grew by only 0.7% from 1991 to 1996, and a growing share of the new money has been earmarked for special education. As a result, in some school districts spending on regular education has actually decreased in the 1990s. This study updates the 1995 EPI report, *Where's the Money Gone?*, which examines school spending for the years 1967-91.

## School Vouchers: Examining the Evidence
Martin Carnoy
Does a voucher threat make schools try harder? A recent Florida study of this education reform approach said yes, but three analyses that replicate its methods show there's no basis for that claim.

## Can Public Schools Learn From Private Schools?
## Case Studies in the Public & Private Sectors
Richard Rothstein, Martin Carnoy, and Luis Benveniste
Rothstein, Carnoy, and Benveniste report on case studies of eight public and eight private schools, which they conducted to determine whether there are any identifiable and transferable private school practices that public schools can adopt in order to improve student outcomes. The evidence from interviews with teachers, administrators, and parents yields a surprising answer, one that should inform our policy debates about school choice, vouchers, public school funding, and other education issues.

## Risky Business: Private Management of Public Schools
Craig E. Richards, Rima Shore, & Max B. Sawicky
Doubts about government efficiency have embraced public education, which in today's global environment is viewed as a critical matter for the nation's youth. *Risky Business* examines one idea for education reform that has attracted the attention of local officials: hiring business firms to manage public schools or public school systems.

## The State of Working America 2002-03
Lawrence Mishel, Jared Bernstein, Heather Boushey
*The State of Working America*, prepared biennially since 1988 by the Economic Policy Institute, sums up the problems and challenges facing American workers. The authors present a wide variety of data on family incomes, taxes, wages, unemployment, wealth, and poverty - data that enable them to closely examine the impact of the economy on the living standards of the American people. This latest edition will be welcomed by journalists, government leaders, researchers, policy makers, professors, and others eager for a comprehensive portrait of the economic well-being of the nation.

# About EPI

**The Economic Policy Institute** was founded in 1986 to widen the debate about policies to achieve healthy economic growth, prosperity, and opportunity.

In the United States today, inequality in wealth, wages, and income remains historically high. Expanding global competition, changes in the nature of work, and rapid technological advances are altering economic reality. Yet many of our policies, attitudes, and institutions are based on assumptions that no longer reflect real world conditions.

With the support of leaders from labor, business, and the foundation world, the Institute has sponsored research and public discussion of a wide variety of topics: trade and fiscal policies; trends in wages, incomes, and prices; education; the causes of the productivity slowdown; labor market problems; rural and urban policies; inflation; state-level economic development strategies; comparative international economic performance; and studies of the overall health of the U.S. manufacturing sector and of specific key industries.

The Institute works with a growing network of innovative economists and other social science researchers in universities and research centers in the U.S. and abroad who are willing to go beyond the conventional wisdom in considering strategies for public policy.

Founding scholars of the Institute include Jeff Faux, distinguished fellow and former president of EPI; Lester Thurow, Sloan School of Management, MIT; Ray Marshall, former U.S. secretary of labor, professor at the LBJ School of Public Affairs, University of Texas; Barry Bluestone, Northeastern University; Robert Reich, former U.S. secretary of labor; and Robert Kuttner, author, editor of *The American Prospect,* and columnist for *Business Week* and the Washington Post Writers Group.

For additional information about the Institute, contact EPI at 1660 L Street NW, Suite 1200, Washington, DC 20036, (202) 775-8810, or visit www.epinet.org.